READ WELL®

Assessment Manual

Placement, Diagnosis, and Prescription

Research Snapshot

REGULAR ASSESSMENT IS THE KEY TO INDIVIDUALLY APPROPRIATE INSTRUCTION

Use the *Read Well* assessment system with fidelity.

Following a review of the research on normal reading development, reading instruction, and factors related to reading failure, the National Research Council (1998) recommended ongoing assessment of word recognition and fluency as a critical component of excellent reading instruction.

"Because the ability to obtain meaning from print depends so strongly on the development of word recognition accuracy and reading fluency, both the latter should be regularly assessed in the classroom, permitting timely and effective instructional response when difficulty or delay is apparent" (Snow, Burns, & Griffin, 1998, p. 7).

Critical Foundations in Primary Reading

Marilyn Sprick, Shelley V. Jones, Richard Dunn, Barbara Gunn

Copyright 2008 (Second Edition) Sopris West Educational Services. All rights reserved.

Permission is granted to the purchasing teacher to reproduce the blackline masters for use in his or her classroom only. No other portion of this work may be reproduced or transmitted in any form or by any means, electronic or mechanical, including photocopying or recording, or by any information storage and retrieval system, without the express written permission of the publisher.

ISBN 13-digit: 978-1-59318-874-0
ISBN 10-digit: 1-59318-874-9

13 12 11 10 09 08   1 2 3 4 5 6

149067

Sopris West™
EDUCATIONAL SERVICES

A Cambium Learning Company

BOSTON, MA • LONGMONT, CO

Table of Contents

SECTION 1 • PLACEMENT ADMINISTRATION 2
    Overview 3
    Managing the Placement Inventory.................................... 5
    Placement Inventory Part 1 7
    Placement Inventory Part 2 14
    Decoding Assessment Guidelines..................................... 16
    Oral Reading Fluency Guidelines 22
    Summary of Placement Inventory.................................... 28
    Placing Students 29

SECTION 2 • PLACEMENT INVENTORY AND FORMS 33
    Placement Inventory Part 1—Administration......................... 34
    Placement Inventory Part 2—Administration......................... 37
    Student Placement Records 43
    Group Placement Form.. 47

SECTION 3 • ONGOING ASSESSMENT........................... 48
    Overview 49
    Managing Assessments 51
    Decoding Assessments, Preludes–Unit 15 54
    Oral Reading Fluency Assessments, Units 16–20...................... 62
    Decoding Diagnosis, Unit 20... 66

SECTION 4 • MAKING DECISIONS............................... 67
    Adjusting Instruction 68
    Using Assessment Results, Preludes A–C............................. 71
    Using Assessment Results, Units 1–5................................. 75
    Using Assessment Results, Units 6–15................................ 78
    Using Assessment Results, Units 16–20............................... 82
    Using a Decoding Diagnosis 86
    Group Record Keeping 88

SECTION 5 • JELL-WELL REVIEWS............................... 92
    Overview and Planning 93
    Menu of Prescriptions 99
    Jell-Well Planner Blackline Master 104

SECTION 6 • ASSESSMENTS AND FORMS....................... 105
    Decoding Assessments, Preludes A–C 106
    Decoding Assessments, Units 1–15 109
    Oral Reading Fluency Assessments, Unit 16–20....................... 124
    Decoding Diagnosis, Unit 20... 129
    Student Assessment Records 130
    Group Assessment Records 142

Introduction

Placement

As all children enter school with their own unique literacy histories and predispositions for learning to read, great care is taken in placing children in instructional groups that will ensure success and a comfortable pace of learning. During the first three weeks of school, each child is assessed for placement in a small group using the *Read Well K* Placement Inventory.

Beginning Small Group Instruction

Small Group instruction begins after Placement Inventories are complete, schedules have been determined, and students are adjusted to their new school routines. Small Group instruction begins after classes have completed *Read Well K* Whole Class Unit 4 and before completing Whole Class Unit 9. (Kindergarten teachers tend to begin Small Group instruction earlier each year that they teach the program.) Daily instruction focuses on the five critical areas of early reading instruction identified by the National Reading Panel (2000): phonemic awareness, phonics, fluency, vocabulary, and comprehension. Instruction is systematic, explicit, rich in content, and mastery based.

Cycle of Assessment and Instruction

Once children are in small groups, careful monitoring ensures that the needs of every individual are met. Regular end-of-unit assessments provide ongoing progress monitoring. Prescriptive teaching follows diagnosis with lesson planning and instruction tailored to the developmental needs of each group and every child. Guidelines for acceleration, early intervention, and group reviews help maximize the progress of each child. Teachers are responsive to the developmental shifts and spurts that occur with young children.

Every Child Deserves to *Read Well*®

SECTION 1
Placement Administration

This section explains how to use the Placement Inventory to group students for success.

Overview	3
Managing the Placement Inventory	5
Placement Inventory Part 1	7
Placement Inventory Part 2	14
Decoding Assessment Guidelines	16
Oral Reading Fluency Guidelines	22
Summary of Placement Inventory	28
Placing Students	29

SECTION 1 Placement Administration

Overview

Placement

The purpose of the *Read Well K* Placement Inventory is to assess whether a student:
- needs to *get ready to read* by starting in the Preludes
- is *ready to read* and can start in Unit 1
- is *already reading* and can start in Unit 6, 10, 16, or *Read Well 1*

Recognizing that schools often have their own battery of extensive and required assessments, the *Read Well K* Placement Inventory quickly but accurately assesses students' skills for preliminary group placement. Once Small Group instruction begins, group membership often changes based on each student's response to instruction.

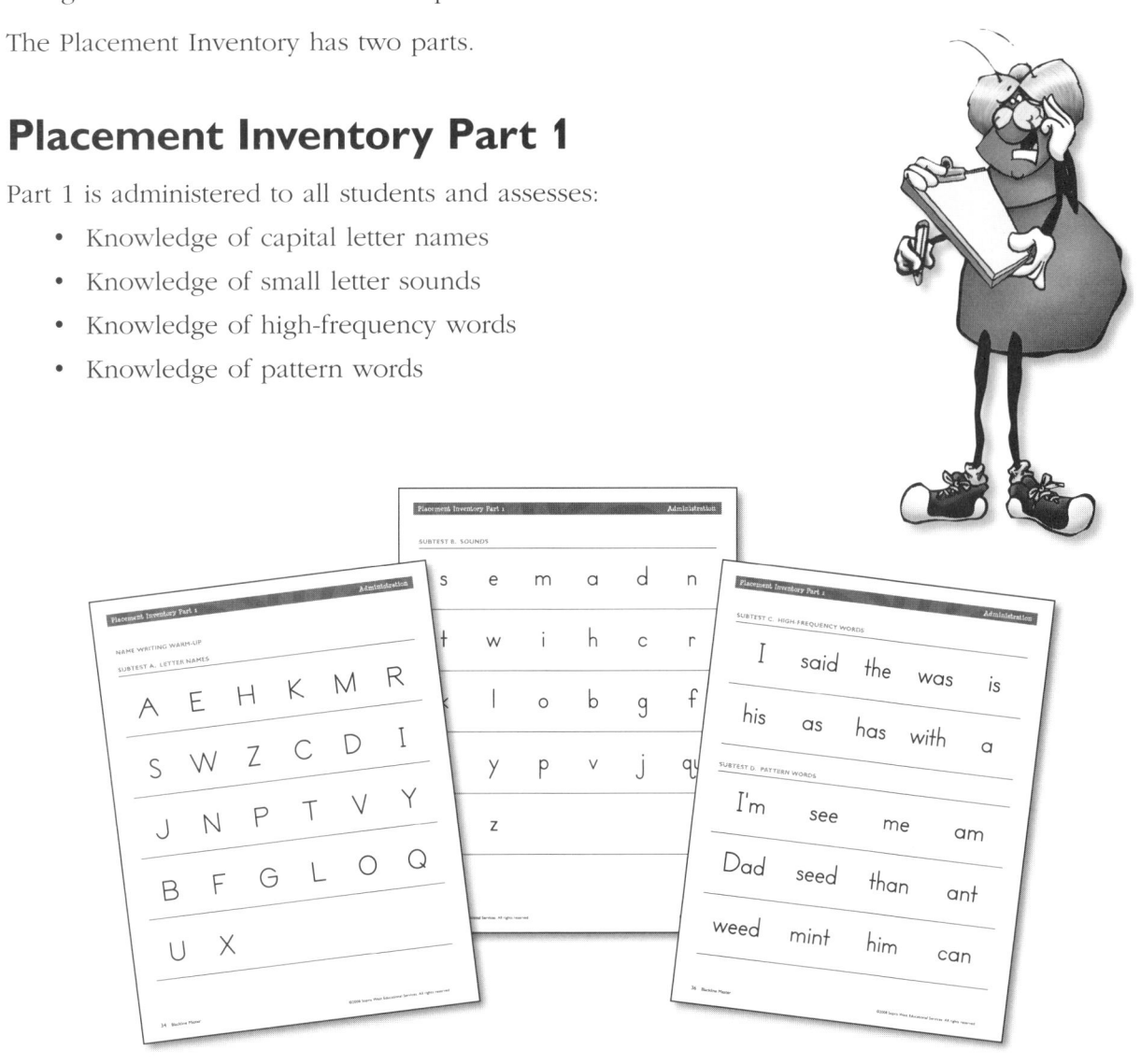

The Placement Inventory has two parts.

Placement Inventory Part 1

Part 1 is administered to all students and assesses:
- Knowledge of capital letter names
- Knowledge of small letter sounds
- Knowledge of high-frequency words
- Knowledge of pattern words

SECTION 1 Placement Administration
Overview

Placement Inventory Part 2

Part 2 is administered only to students who are able to identify 17 or more letters and sounds and read nine or more words (minimum total score of 26) from Part 1. Part 2 consists of selected end-of-unit *Read Well K* Decoding Assessments and Oral Reading Fluency Assessments.

Part 2 includes Decoding Assessments from Units 1, 5, 9, and 15. The assessments measure:

- Knowledge of sounds
- Knowledge of blending
- Knowledge of irregular words
- Ability to read sentences accurately and with fluency

If students score Strong Passes, they proceed to the Oral Reading Fluency Assessment from Unit 20.
This assessment measures:

- Knowledge of Tricky Words
- Oral reading fluency

Placement Guidelines

Children can place in many potential entry points.

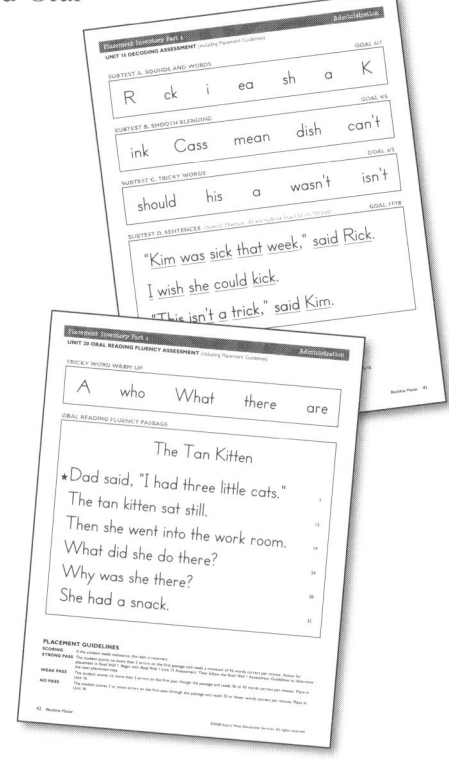

ENTRY	PLACEMENT GUIDELINES
• Prelude A • Unit 1 • Unit 6 • Unit 10 • Unit 16 • *Read Well 1*	**Place students conservatively.** Once instruction begins, students can be moved easily from one group to the next. If in doubt, place students in the lowest appropriate group.

Once all Placement Inventories are completed, compromises can be made to accommodate group placement, but no child should ever be placed at a higher level than his or her score indicates. All children should experience success from the start of instruction.

SECTION 1 Placement Administration

Managing the Placement Inventory

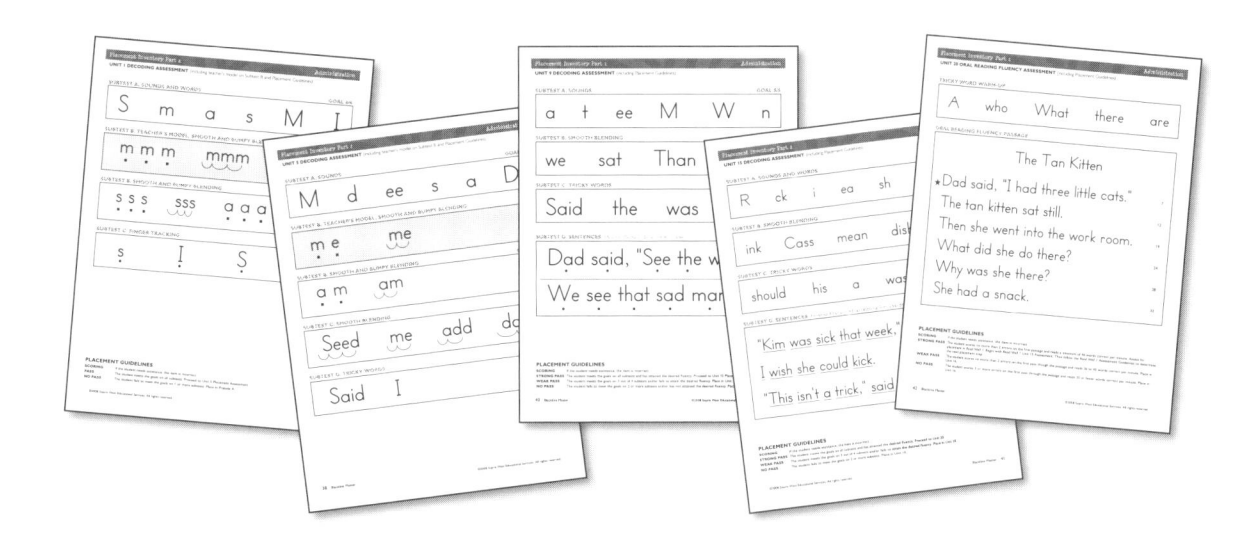

When to Administer

The Placement Inventory should be administered to all kindergarten students during the first three weeks of school. If you don't begin Small Group instruction until the eighth week of school or later, consider re-administering the Placement Inventory. The Placement Inventory should also be administered to kindergarten transfer students any time during the year and to remedial students any time *Read Well K* is considered as a program option.

Who Administers

The first weeks of school are a time of newness and uncertainty for young children. Because classroom teachers are fully occupied meeting the needs of their students, assessments should be administered outside of class time or by other trained professionals. Because each school varies in its opening routines and resources, consider the following options:

- Have an assessment team assess individual students while the teacher continues teaching.
- Have another trained professional administer the Placement Inventory while a parent conferences with the teacher.
- Have a trained professional administer the Placement Inventory at the time the student registers.

SECTION 1 Placement Administration
Managing the Placement Inventory

Materials Preparation

1. Make one copy per student of the Student Placement Record, Part 1 (page 43). This form is used to record and score student responses. Keep the Student Placement Record, Part 1 in each student's file or portfolio as a pretest measure.

2. Make additional copies of the Student Placement Record, Part 2 (pages 44–46). Part 2 will only be used with children who score 26 or more on Part 1. The student record forms for Part 2 can be stapled to Part 1, as needed.

3. For each person who will administer the Placement Inventory, make one copy of the Placement Inventory administration forms (pages 34–42). You may wish to laminate the administration pages or place the pages in plastic sheet protectors.

4. Obtain stopwatches. The assessments in Part 2 of the Placement Inventory for Units 9, 15, and 20 include timings to track students' word-reading fluency.

5. Place the Student Placement Record forms on clipboards for each person administering the Placement Inventory.

6. Set up a quiet place to administer the Placement Inventory. Students should be seated at a table.

SECTION 1 Placement Administration

Placement Inventory Part 1

Administration Guidelines

Part 1 of the Placement Inventory is composed of a warm-up activity and four subtests: letter names, letter sounds, high-frequency words, and pattern words.

When administering the Placement Inventory:

- Assess each child individually, away from others.

- Record student responses on the Student Placement Record, Part 1. Record a *plus* for each correct response and a *minus* for each incorrect response.

- For each assessment item, wait three seconds. If the student does not respond, struggles, or gives an incorrect response, gently tell the student the letter name, sound, or word and score the item as incorrect. Then encourage the student to copy your response.

    Say something like:
    > That's /ăăă/.
    > Say it with me. /ăăă/
    > That's right. That letter says /ăăă/.

    With this simple procedure, children view this early assessment as a learning experience, rather than a test.

- On each subtest, stop if the student makes five consecutive errors. Point to the remaining rows and ask the student if he or she knows any of the letters, sounds, or words. Give credit for any correct responses.

If your district has a Letter Name Assessment and Letter Sound Assessment, the results of the district assessments can be used for these subtests.

If you wish to assess both capital letter names and sounds and small letter names and sounds, Subtests A and B can be scored twice using two different colors.

For placement purposes, we have found that the additional information attained by assessing both capital and small letter names and sounds is *not* necessary; however, for pre/post test comparisons, additional information is always of value.

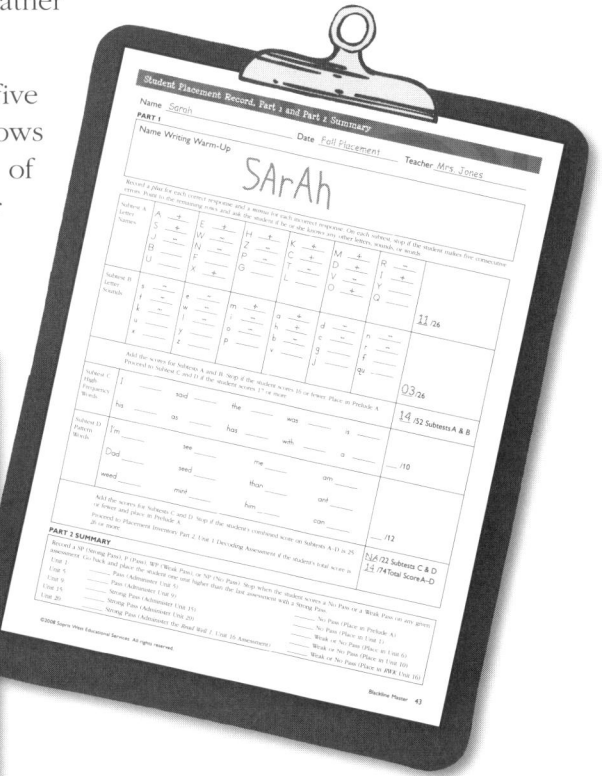

SECTION 1 Placement Administration
Placement Inventory Part 1

How to Administer the Subtests

Name Writing Warm-Up

Name writing provides an informal assessment of a student's literacy background.

Point to the box at the top of the Student Placement Record and have the student write his or her name.

Say something like:

> Can you write your name for me?

If the student:

- **Has difficulty, compliment the student on something she or he can do.**

    Say something like:

    > That's great! You can write a T for *Tatum*.

- **Is able to write his or her first name with ease,** ask the student to write his or her last name.

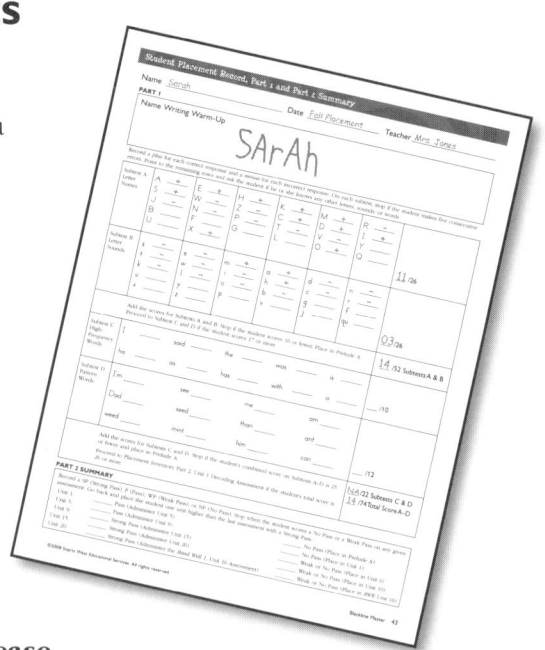

Subtest A. Letter Names

Have the student identify the letter names.

With the student:

Point to the first letter in Subtest A. Say something like:

> I'd like you to point to each letter and say its name.

If the student:

- **Does not say the letter name within three seconds**, score as incorrect. Tell the student the letter name and encourage the student to say the letter name.

    > That's the letter M. What letter is that? (M)
    > That's right.

- **Says the letter sound**, say something like:

    > That's the letter sound.
    > Can you tell me the letter name?

    Score only the letter name as a correct response.

Reproducible Placement Inventory Part 1, Subtest A available on page 34.

SECTION 1 Placement Administration

Placement Inventory Part 1

Subtest B. Sounds

Have the student identify the letter sounds.

With the student:
Point to the first letter in Subtest B. Say something like:

> I'd like you to point to each letter and tell me its sound.

If the student:

- **Does not say the letter sound within three seconds**, score as incorrect. Tell the student the letter sound and encourage him or her to say the letter sound.

- **Says the letter name**, say:

  > That's the letter name. Do you know its sound?

  Score only the sound as a correct response.

- **Says the letter name for a vowel** (the long vowel sound), say:

  > Yes, can you tell me another sound for that letter?

  Score only the short sounds (as in: ant, in, end, on, and up) as correct.

- **Says the soft sound for g (as in giant) or for c (as in circus)**, say:

  > Yes, can you tell me another sound for that letter?

  Score only the hard sounds as correct (e.g., /g/ as in gorilla and /k/ as in cat).

- **Co-articulates a quick (or stop) sound consonant with a vowel sound (e.g., /dŭh/, rather than /d/)**. Score the response as correct, but note the pronunciation on the scoring sheet. (For ease of blending, the quick pronunciation of the stop sounds will be taught and assessed during instruction.)

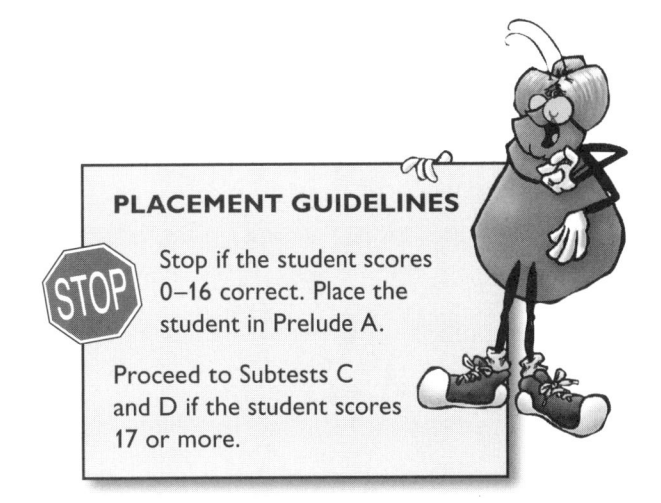

Reproducible Placement Inventory Part 1, Subtest B available on page 35.

PLACEMENT GUIDELINES

Stop if the student scores 0–16 correct. Place the student in Prelude A.

Proceed to Subtests C and D if the student scores 17 or more.

SECTION 1 Placement Administration
Placement Inventory Part 1

Subtest C. High-Frequency Words

With the student:
Have the student read the words. Point to the first word in Subtest C. Say something like:

> You can read letter names and sounds. I'd like to see if you can read words too. Point to each word and tell me what you think it says.

If the student:

- **Reads a word as it is pronounced within three seconds**, score the response as correct.

- **Does not attempt a word within three seconds**, score the response as incorrect. Tell the student the word and encourage him or her to say the word.

- **Sounds out a word as it looks, but not as it is pronounced**, say:

  > How do you say that word?

  If the student then pronounces the word correctly, score the response as correct. For example, if a student sounds out "is" as follows: /ĭĭĭsss/, you would say:

  > How do you say that word?

  If a student says /ĭz/, score the response as correct.

Subtest D. Pattern Words

With the student:
Have the student read the words. Point to the first row of words in Subtest D. Say something like:

> I'd like to see if you can read any of these. Point to the first word and see if you can tell me what it says.

If the student:

- **Sounds out a word correctly**, score the response as correct.

- **Struggles with the word or does not attempt a word within three seconds**, score as incorrect.

  Tell the student the word and encourage the student to say the word.

  > That's a hard word. It says *I'm*. Tell me the word. (I'm)

PLACEMENT GUIDELINES

Stop if the student's total score on Subtests A–D is 25 or less. Place the student in Prelude A.

Proceed to Part 2 if the student's total score on Subtests A–D is 26 or more.

SECTION 1 **Placement Administration**

Placement Inventory Part 1

Placement Inventory Part 1 — Administration

SUBTEST C. HIGH-FREQUENCY WORDS

| I | said | the | was | is |

| his | as | has | with | a |

Subtest C. High-Frequency Words

SUBTEST D. PATTERN WORDS

| I'm | see | me | am |

| Dad | seed | than | ant |

| weed | mint | him | can |

Subtest D. Pattern Words

36 Blackline Master   ©2008 Sopris West Educational Services. All rights reserved.

Reproducible Placement Inventory Part 1, Subtests C and D available on page 36.

SECTION 1 — Placement Administration
Placement Inventory Part 1

Sarah's Example

Warm-Up

Sarah is able to write her first name, mixing capital letters and small letters. She is not able to write her last name.

Subtests A and B

Sarah knows 11 letter names. She knows three sounds, the three sounds introduced in the first three units of Whole Class instruction.

Subtests C and D

Subtests C and D were not administered, because Sarah scored 16 or fewer on the subtests for Letter Names and Sounds.

Total Score

Sarah's total score is 14.

Part 2 of the Placement Inventory is not administered, because Sarah scored 25 or fewer on Part 1 of the Placement Inventory. Sarah places in Prelude A, where she will get ready to learn to read.

Student Placement Record, Part 1 and Part 2 Summary

Name: Sarah   Date: Fall Placement   Teacher: Mrs. Jones

PART 1

Name Writing Warm-Up: **SArAh**

Record a *plus* for each correct response and a *minus* for each incorrect response. On each subtest, stop if the student makes five consecutive errors. Point to the remaining rows and ask the student if he or she knows any other letters, sounds, or words.

Subtest A Letter Names						
A +	E +	H +	K +	M +	R −	
S +	W −	Z −	C +	D +	I +	
J −	N −	P −	T −	V −	Y −	
B −	F −	G −	L −	O +	Q −	
U −	X +					**11** /26

Subtest B Letter Sounds						
s −	e −	m +	a +	d −	n −	
t −	w −	i −	h +	c −	r −	
k −	l −	o −	b −	g −	f −	
u −	y −	p −	v −	j −	qu −	
x −	z −					**03** /26

Add the scores for Subtests A and B. Stop if the student scores 16 or fewer. Place in Prelude A. Proceed to Subtest C and D if the student scores 17 or more.   **14** /52 Subtests A & B

Subtest C High-Frequency Words
I ___   said ___   the ___   was ___   is ___
his ___   as ___   has ___   with ___   a ___   ___ /10

Subtest D Pattern Words
I'm ___   see ___   me ___   am ___
Dad ___   seed ___   than ___   ant ___
weed ___   mint ___   him ___   can ___   ___ /12

Add the scores for Subtests C and D. Stop if the student's combined score on Subtests A–D is 25 or fewer and place in Prelude A.   **NA** /22 Subtests C & D
Proceed to Placement Inventory Part 2, Unit 1 Decoding Assessment if the student's total score is 26 or more.   **14** /74 Total Score A–D

PART 2 SUMMARY

Record a SP (Strong Pass), P (Pass), WP (Weak Pass), or NP (No Pass). Stop when the student scores a No Pass or a Weak Pass on any given assessment. Go back and place the student one unit higher than the last assessment with a Strong Pass.

- Unit 1: _____ Pass (Administer Unit 5)   _____ No Pass (Place in Prelude A)
- Unit 5: _____ Pass (Administer Unit 9)   _____ No Pass (Place in Unit 1)
- Unit 9: _____ Strong Pass (Administer Unit 15)   _____ Weak or No Pass (Place in Unit 6)
- Unit 15: _____ Strong Pass (Administer Unit 20)   _____ Weak or No Pass (Place in Unit 10)
- Unit 20: _____ Strong Pass (Administer the *Read Well 1*, Unit 16 Assessment)   _____ Weak or No Pass (Place in *RWK* Unit 16)

©2008 Sopris West Educational Services. All rights reserved.   Blackline Master 43

Reproducible Student Placement Record, Part 1 and Part 2 Summary available on page 43.

SECTION 1 Placement Administration

Placement Inventory Part 1

Jeffery's Example

Warm-Up

Jeffery is able to write his first name and last name, using appropriate capital and small letters.

Subtests A and B

Jeffery demonstrated knowledge of 26 letter names and 23 sounds. Jeffery scored a total of 49 on Subtests A and B, so he was given Subtests C and D.

Subtests C and D

Jeffery is able to read 10 high-frequency words and 12 pattern words. His combined score on Subtests C and D is 22.

Placement Inventory Part 1, Total Score

Jeffery's total score is 71. Jeffery will go on to Part 2 of the Placement Inventory. Jeffery's score on Part 1 may be used to help place him with students who most closely match his skills at the time of testing.

Student Placement Record, Part 1 and Part 2 Summary

Name: Jeffery Date: Fall Placement Teacher: Mr. Duncan

PART 1

Name Writing Warm-Up: *Jeffery Johnson*

Record a *plus* for each correct response and a *minus* for each incorrect response. On each subtest, stop if the student makes five consecutive errors. Point to the remaining rows and ask the student if he or she knows any other letters, sounds, or words.

Subtest A Letter Names												
A +	E +	H +	K +	M +	R +							
S +	W +	Z +	C +	D +	I +							
J +	N +	P +	T +	V +	Y +							
B +	F +	G +	L +	O +	Q +							**26**/26
U +	X +											

Subtest B Letter Sounds							
s +	e +	m +	a +	d +	n +		
t +	w +	i +	h +	c +	r +		
k +	l +	o +	b +	g +	f +		
u +	y −	p +	v +	j +	qu −		**23**/26
x −	z +						

Add the scores for Subtests A and B. Stop if the student scores 16 or fewer. Place in Prelude A. Proceed to Subtest C and D if the student scores 17 or more.   **49**/52 Subtests A & B

Subtest C High-Frequency Words						
I +	said +	the +	was +	is +		
his +	as +	has +	with +	a +		**10**/10

Subtest D Pattern Words				
I'm +	see +	me +	am +	
Dad +	seed +	than +	ant +	
weed +	mint +	him +	can +	**12**/12

Add the scores for Subtests C and D. Stop if the student's combined score on Subtests A–D is 25 or fewer and place in Prelude A.   **22**/22 Subtests C & D
Proceed to Placement Inventory Part 2, Unit 1 Decoding Assessment if the student's total score is 26 or more.   **71**/74 Total Score A–D

PART 2 SUMMARY

Record a SP (Strong Pass), P (Pass), WP (Weak Pass), or NP (No Pass). Stop when the student scores a No Pass or a Weak Pass on any given assessment. Go back and place the student one unit higher than the last assessment with a Strong Pass.

- Unit 1: __P__ Pass (Administer Unit 5) ____ No Pass (Place in Prelude A)
- Unit 5: __P__ Pass (Administer Unit 9) ____ No Pass (Place in Unit 1)
- Unit 9: __SP__ Strong Pass (Administer Unit 15) ____ Weak or No Pass (Place in Unit 6)
- Unit 15: ____ Strong Pass (Administer Unit 20) __NP__ Weak or No Pass (Place in Unit 10)
- Unit 20: ____ Strong Pass (Administer the *Read Well 1*, Unit 16 Assessment) ____ Weak or No Pass (Place in *RWK* Unit 16)

©2008 Sopris West Educational Services. All rights reserved.   Blackline Master 43

Reproducible Student Placement Record, Part 1 and Part 2 Summary available on page 43.

SECTION 1 Placement Administration

Placement Inventory Part 2

Administration Guidelines

Part 2 of the Placement Inventory assesses whether a child is *ready to read* and can skip the Preludes and begin instruction at Unit 1 or is *already reading* and should start in Unit 6, 10, or 16. In some cases, a student may be ready for placement in *Read Well 1*.

- Children who enter the program with a literacy background and/or a receptiveness to literacy instruction will likely place in *Read Well K* Unit 1.
- Children who are already beginning to read will place in Unit 6 or higher.
- Some children may know several high-frequency words by sight but lack the skills to read pattern words. Such students will place in Unit 1 but will progress rapidly through the early units.

SECTION 1: Placement Administration

Placement Inventory Part 2

When administering the Placement Inventory:
- Assess each child individually, away from others.
- Follow the schedule below until a student scores a Weak Pass or a No Pass on any given assessment.
- Record student responses on the Student Placement Record Part 2.

ADMINISTRATION SCHEDULE

Administer test for...	If the student scores a...	Then...
Unit 1	No Pass / Pass	Place in Prelude A / Administer Unit 5
Unit 5	No Pass / Pass	Place in Unit 1 / Administer Unit 9
Unit 9	Weak or No Pass / Strong Pass	Place in Unit 6 / Administer Unit 15
Unit 15	Weak or No Pass / Strong Pass	Place in Unit 10 / Administer Unit 20
Unit 20	Weak or No Pass / Strong Pass	Place in Unit 16 / Assess for placement in *Read Well 1*

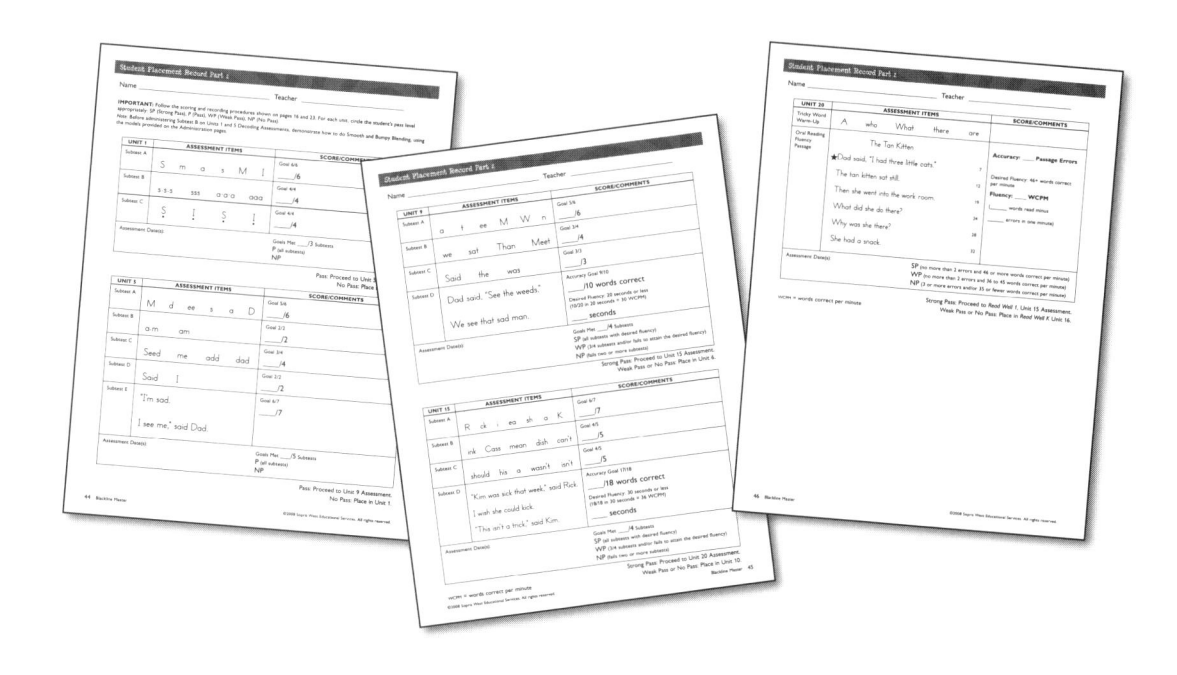

SECTION 1 Placement Administration
Placement Inventory Part 2

Decoding Assessment Guidelines

Part 2 of the Placement Inventory begins with end-of-the-unit Decoding Assessments for Units 1, 5, 9, and 15. These subtests assess a student's skills with letter sounds, Smooth and Bumpy Blending, Tricky Words, and sentence reading. These subtests are scored on the Student Placement Record Part 2. Code errors as shown in the chart.

PROCEDURES AND SCORING FOR ALL SUBTESTS		
If the student . . .	**Then . . .**	**Record . . .**
Needs Assistance	Wait three seconds. Gently tell the student the correct response, draw a line through the item, and write an "A" for "assisted." Score as an incorrect response.	Incorrect M d̶(A) ee s a D
Mispronounces	Draw a line through the word. Record what the student said and score as an incorrect response.	Incorrect s̶o̶d̶(sad) was sees
Fails to Blend Smoothly (Smooth and Bumpy Blending Subtest)	*Special Note:* For the Placement Inventory, the Smooth and Bumpy Blending Subtest is preceded by a teacher demonstration of Smooth and Bumpy Blending. If the student fails to blend smoothly (e.g., pauses or stops between sounds), draw a line through the item. Rewrite the word and draw dashes between sounds to indicate where the student paused. Score as an incorrect response.	Incorrect S̶e̶e̶d̶ (s-ee-d) me add d̶a̶d̶ (d-ad)
Self-Corrects	If the student spontaneously self-corrects, write "SC," so that you do not count the error. If the student requires more than two attempts, score as an incorrect response.	Incorrect Correct Does/Dan/Did sun (SC) D̶i̶d̶ Tim sit in the sand?

SECTION 1 — Placement Administration

Placement Inventory Part 2

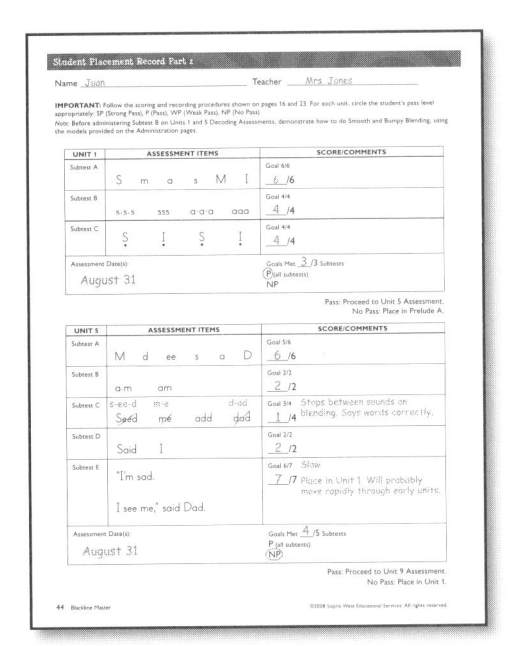

Student Placement Record Part 2 Scoring Sample

Record errors on the Student Placement Record Part 2 while administering the assessment.

Reproducible Student Placement Records Part 2, available on pages 44–46.

For Units 9, 15, and 20, time Subtest D in each unit.

TIMED READINGS

As the student begins reading:

1. Start the stopwatch.
2. Be sure to pronounce words not read within three seconds and prompt the student to keep reading.
3. Score as indicated on page 16. However, if a student sounds out a word (whether smooth or bumpy), score as a correct response. Sounding out is reflected in the fluency score.

Transfer assessment scores SP (Strong Pass), P (Pass), WP (Weak Pass), and NP (No Pass), as appropriate, onto the Student Placement Record, Part 1 and Part 2 Summary.

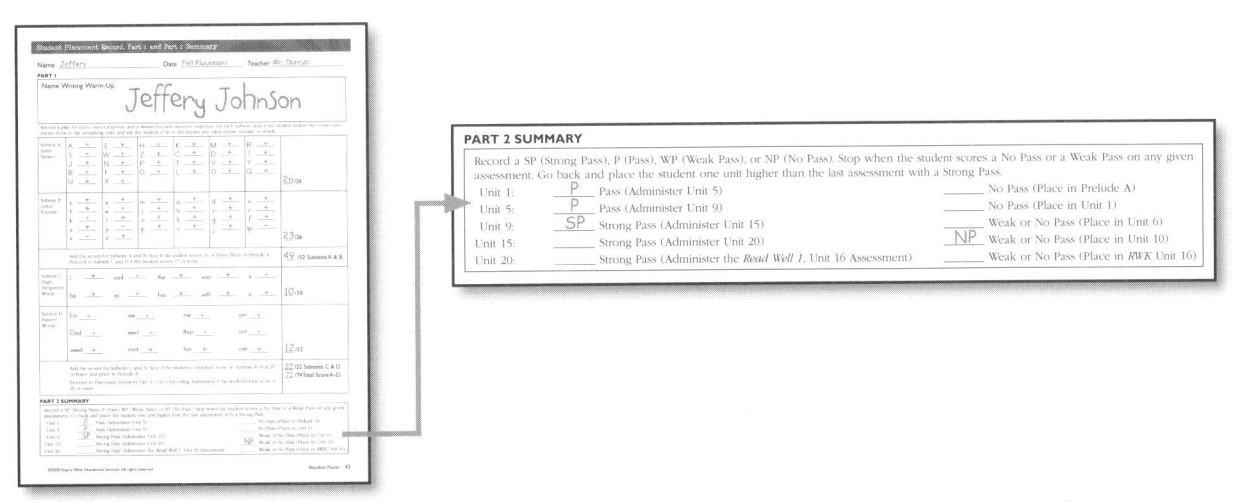

Continue assessing until the student scores a Weak Pass or No Pass. Go back and place the student one unit higher than the last unit with a Strong Pass or Pass. (See chart on page 15.)

17

SECTION 1 Placement Administration
Placement Inventory Part 2

How to Administer Units 1 and 5
(Unit 1 has only Subtest A and Subtest B.)

Record student responses on Part 2 of the Student Placement Record, Part 1 and Part 2 Summary.

Subtest A. Sounds

Tell the student to point to each item and say the sound. Say something like:

Touch under the first sound. Tell me the sound. (/mmm/)
Touch under the next sound. Tell me the sound. (/d/)

Subtest B. Smooth and Bumpy Blending

Demonstrate Smooth and Bumpy Blending, using the examples on the Administration Forms for Unit 1 and Unit 5.

UNIT 1	UNIT 5
Watch and listen to me do Bumpy Blending. **Touch under each letter.** /m/ pause /m/ pause /m/ Now watch and listen to me do Smooth Blending. **Loop under each letter.** /mmmmmm/	Watch and listen to me do Bumpy Blending. **Touch under each letter.** /m/ pause /ē/ Now watch and listen to me do Smooth Blending. **Loop under each letter.** /mmmēēē/

Following your model, say something like:

Now you get to do Bumpy Blending. You can follow my finger or point by yourself.
Touch the dot under the first sound. Do Bumpy Blending. (/ă/ pause /m/)
Now do Smooth Blending. Put your finger at the beginning of the first loop.
Do Smooth Blending. (/ăăămmm/)
Tell me the word. (ăm)

Subtest C. Smooth Blending

Tell the student to do Smooth Blending of each word. Say something like:

You get to do Smooth Blending. Put your finger at the beginning of the first loop.
Do Smooth Blending. (/sssēēēd/)
Tell me the word. (Seed)

Subtest D. Tricky Words

Tell the student to point to each word and read the word.

Put your finger under the first Tricky Word.
Tell me the word. (Said)

SECTION 1 — Placement Administration

Placement Inventory Part 2

Subtest E. Sentences

Tell the student to point to the first word in the sentence and then read the sentence. Say something like:

> You get to read sentences.
>
> Put your finger under the first word and start when you're ready.

Placement Inventory Part 2 — Administration

UNIT 5 DECODING ASSESSMENT (including teacher's model on Subtest B and Placement Guidelines)

SUBTEST A. SOUNDS — GOAL 5/6

M d ee s a D

SUBTEST B. TEACHER'S MODEL, SMOOTH AND BUMPY BLENDING

m e   me

SUBTEST B. SMOOTH AND BUMPY BLENDING — GOAL 2/2

a m   am

SUBTEST C. SMOOTH BLENDING — GOAL 3/4

Seed   me   add   dad

SUBTEST D. TRICKY WORDS — GOAL 2/2

Said   I

(continued)

Reproducible Placement Inventory Part 2, Unit 5 Decoding Assessment available on pages 38–39.

Placement Inventory Part 2 — Administration

UNIT 5 DECODING ASSESSMENT *(continued)*

SUBTEST E. SENTENCES — GOAL 6/7

"I'm sad.

I see me," said Dad.

SECTION 1 Placement Administration
Placement Inventory Part 2

How to Administer Units 9 and 15

Following is a sample script from Unit 15.

Subtest A. Sounds

Tell the student to point to each item and say the sound. Say something like:

Touch under the first sound. Read the sound. (/rrr/)

Subtest B. Smooth Blending

Tell the student to do Smooth Blending of each word.

You get to do Smooth Blending. Remember, you want to really stretch out the words.
Do Smooth Blending. (/iiinnnk/)
Tell me the word. (ink)

Subtest C. Tricky Words

Tell the student to point to each word and read the word.

Put your finger under the first Tricky Word.
Tell me the word. (should)

Subtest D. Sentences

- Tell the student to point to the first word in the sentence and then read the sentence. Say something like:

  You get to read sentences.
  Put your finger under the first word and start when you're ready.

- Begin timing when the student reads the first word in the sentence.
- If the student does not pronounce a word within three seconds, quietly tell the student the word and have the student continue.
- Stop timing after the student reads the last word in the last sentence.
- Record the number of seconds to completion.

SECTION 1 Placement Administration

Placement Inventory Part 2

Placement Inventory Part 2 — Administration

UNIT 15 DECODING ASSESSMENT (including Placement Guidelines)

SUBTEST A. SOUNDS AND WORDS — GOAL 6/7

| R | ck | i | ea | sh | a | K |

SUBTEST B. SMOOTH BLENDING — GOAL 4/5

| ink | Cass | mean | dish | can't |

SUBTEST C. TRICKY WORDS — GOAL 4/5

| should | his | a | wasn't | isn't |

SUBTEST D. SENTENCES Desired Fluency: 30 seconds or less (34–36 WCPM) — GOAL 17/18

"Kim was sick that week," said Rick.
I wish she could kick.
"This isn't a trick," said Kim.

PLACEMENT GUIDELINES
- **SCORING** — If the student needs assistance, the item is incorrect.
- **STRONG PASS** — The student meets the goals on all subtests and has attained the desired flu...
- **WEAK PASS** — The student meets the goals on 3 out of 4 subtests and/or fails to attain...
- **NO PASS** — The student fails to meet the goals on 2 or more subtests. Place in Unit 10.

©2008 Sopris West Educational Services. All rights reserved.

Student Placement Record Part 2

Name _____ Teacher _____

UNIT 9	ASSESSMENT ITEMS	SCORE/COMMENTS
Subtest A	a t ee M W n	Goal 5/6 ____/6
Subtest B	we sat Than Meet	Goal 3/4 ____/4
Subtest C	Said the was	Goal 3/3 ____/3
Subtest D	Dad said, "See the weeds." We see that sad man.	Accuracy Goal 9/10 ____/10 words correct Desired Fluency: 20 seconds or less (10/20 in 20 seconds = 30 WCPM) ____ seconds
Assessment Date(s):		Goals Met ____/4 Subtests SP (all subtests with desired fluency) WP (3/4 subtests and/or fails to attain the desired fluency) NP (fails two or more subtests)

Strong Pass: Proceed to Unit 15 Assessment.
Weak Pass or No Pass: Place in Unit 6.

UNIT 15	ASSESSMENT ITEMS	SCORE/COMMENTS
Subtest A	R ck i ea sh a K	Goal 6/7 ____/7
Subtest B	ink Cass mean dish can't	Goal 4/5 ____/5
Subtest C	should his a wasn't isn't	Goal 4/5 ____/5
Subtest D	"Kim was sick that week," said Rick. I wish she could kick. "This isn't a trick," said Kim.	Accuracy Goal 17/18 ____/18 words correct Desired Fluency: 30 seconds or less (18/18 in 30 seconds = 36 WCPM) ____ seconds
Assessment Date(s):		Goals Met ____/4 Subtests SP (all subtests with desired fluency) WP (3/4 subtests and/or fails to attain the desired fluency) NP (fails two or more subtests)

Strong Pass: Proceed to Unit 20 Assessment.
Weak Pass or No Pass: Place in Unit 10.

WCPM = words correct per minute
©2008 Sopris West Educational Services. All rights reserved.
Blackline Master 45

Sample of completed Student Replacement Record, Part 2.

SECTION 1 Placement Administration
Placement Inventory Part 2

Oral Reading Fluency Guidelines

Part 2 of the Placement Inventory also includes an end-of-the-unit Oral Reading Fluency Assessment for Unit 20. This assessment begins with an unscored and untimed Tricky Word warm-up, followed by an Oral Reading Fluency Passage scored for accuracy and fluency.

Tricky Word Warm-Up

Have the student point to and read each word. Mark errors on the Student Assessment Record.

Oral Reading Fluency Passage

Passing criteria include two measures for the *same* passage reading.

- **Accuracy:** Number of errors made for the passage on the first time through
  The accuracy score provides a measure of a student's informal reading level (independent, instructional, or frustration). As passage length increases, students are gradually required to be at an independent level to pass an assessment (98–100% accuracy).
- **Oral Reading Fluency:** Words correct per minute (WCPM)
  WCPM provides a measure of accuracy and speed. WCPM is the words read in one minute, minus errors for that minute.

Administering the Oral Reading Fluency Subtest

1. Have the student read the title. The title provides an unscored warm-up.

2. Start timing the passage at the ★. Mark errors using the diagnostic scoring on page 23. Have the student complete the passage and continue reading for a full 60 seconds.
   - If the student has not completed the passage by the end of 60 seconds, make a single slash (/) at the point the student reached.
   - If the student finishes the passage before 60 seconds have passed, have the student go back to the ★ and keep reading. Stop the student at 60 seconds and make a double slash (//). On the second pass, mark errors differently (e.g., ✓).

Determining Accuracy and Oral Reading Fluency Scores

1. **For the accuracy score,** count the number of errors made in the passage.
   - If the student required more than 60 seconds to complete the passage, count errors for the whole passage.
   - If the student read the passage more than once, count errors only for the first time through.

2. **For the oral reading fluency score,** count the number of words read to the double or single slash. Subtract errors made during the 60-second reading.

SECTION 1 Placement Administration

Placement Inventory Part 2

DIAGNOSTIC SCORING FOR UNIT 20

If the student...	Then...	Record...
Needs Assistance	Wait three seconds. Gently tell the student the correct response, draw a line through the item, and write an "A" for "assisted." Score as an incorrect response.	Incorrect The tan kitten sat st~~ill~~. ⁿᴬ
Mispronounces a Word	Draw a line through the item. Record what the student said. Score as an incorrect response.	Incorrect I h~~ad~~ three little cats. (have)
Omits a Word or Word Part	Circle the omission. Score as an incorrect response.	Incorrect Then she went in(to) the work room.
Inserts a Word	Write what the student said, using a caret to show where the student inserted the word.	Incorrect What did she do ^in there?
Self-Corrects	If a student spontaneously self-corrects, write "SC" and score as a correct response.	Correct What/Why ˢᶜ Why was she there?
	If the student requires more than two attempts, score as an incorrect response.	Incorrect What/When/Why Why was she there?
Repeats Words	Underline repeated words.	Correct <u>What</u> did she do there?
Reverses Words	Draw a line around the words as shown.	Correct The tan kitten sat⌒still.

SECOND TIME THROUGH

| Any Error | Make a ✓ over each word | ✓
She had a snack. |

23

SECTION 1: Placement Administration

Placement Inventory Part 2

Georgina's Example

Student Placement Record Part 2

Name: _Georgina_   Teacher: _Mrs. Jones_

UNIT 20	ASSESSMENT ITEMS	SCORE/COMMENTS
Tricky Word Warm-Up	A who What there are	
Oral Reading Fluency Passage	The Tan Kitten ★Dad said, "I ~~had~~ (have) three little cats." 7 The tan kitten sat still. 12 Then she went <u>into</u> the work room. 19 What did she do there? 24 ~~Why~~ What SC was she there? / 28 She had a ~~snack~~ (treat). 32	**Accuracy:** _2_ Passage Errors Desired Fluency: 46+ words correct per minute **Fluency:** _27_ **WCPM** (_28_ words read minus _1_ errors in one minute)
Assessment Date(s):	SP (no more than 2 errors and 46 or more words correct per minute) WP (no more than 2 errors and 36 to 45 words correct per minute) (NP) (3 or more errors and/or 35 or fewer words correct per minute)	

WCPM = words correct per minute

Strong Pass: Proceed to *Read Well 1*, Unit 15 Assessment.
Weak Pass or No Pass: Place in *Read Well K* Unit 16.

Georgina's Score

Georgina read to the word "there" in one minute (/).

Her passage errors were "had" and "snack."

Georgina's accuracy score is two passage errors.

To calculate WCPM, only the word "had" is counted as an error because it was made during the one-minute timing. Georgina read 28 words in one minute, minus one error. Her fluency score is 27 WCPM.

Reproducible Student Placement Record available on page 46.

SECTION 1 — Placement Administration

Placement Inventory Part 2

Brandon's Example

Brandon's Score

Brandon read the whole passage and then went back to the star and read again to "there" in one minute. (//)

Brandon made an error on "kitten" the first time he read the passage. His accuracy score is one passage error.

The second time Brandon read the passage, he missed "work" (✓). Brandon's WCPM is calculated by adding 32 (first reading) plus 28 (second reading), minus the two errors made during the one-minute timing (32+28-2). Brandon's fluency score is 58 WCPM.

Student Placement Record Part 2

Name: Brandon   Teacher: Mr. Duncan

UNIT 20	ASSESSMENT ITEMS	SCORE/COMMENTS
Tricky Word Warm-Up	A who What there are	
Oral Reading Fluency Passage	The Tan Kitten ★Dad said, "I had three little cats." 7 The tan ~~kitten~~ *cat* sat still. 12 Then she went into the work✓ room. 19 ~~What~~ *Why SC* did she do there? 24 Why was she there?// 28 She had a snack. 32	Accuracy: __1__ Passage Errors Desired Fluency: 46+ words correct per minute Fluency: __58__ WCPM (__60__ words read minus __2__ errors in one minute)

Assessment Date(s): _____

(SP) (no more than 2 errors and 46 or more words correct per minute)
WP (no more than 2 errors and 36 to 45 words correct per minute)
NP (3 or more errors and/or 35 or fewer words correct per minute)

WCPM = words correct per minute

Strong Pass: Proceed to *Read Well 1*, Unit 15 Assessment.
Weak Pass or No Pass: Place in *Read Well K* Unit 16.

Reproducible Student Placement Record available on page 46.

SECTION 1 Placement Administration
Placement Inventory Part 2

How to Administer Unit 20

The following is a sample script for Unit 20.

Tricky Word Warm-Up

Tell the student to point to each item and say the word. Say something like:

> Touch under the first word. Read the word.

Oral Reading Fluency

- Tell the student to point to the first word in the title. Say:

   > Read the title of the story. What do you think the story is going to be about?

- Have the student point to the first word in the passage. Have the student read the complete passage and continue reading for 60 seconds. Say something like:

   > Read the story to me. Please track the words with your finger, so I can see where you are reading. Put your finger under the first word. Begin whenever you are ready.

- If time remains at the end of the passage, have the student go back to the ★ and keep reading until 60 seconds have passed. Say something like:

   > Wow! Go back to the star and keep reading.

As the student reads, code any errors using the general scoring procedures shown on page 23.

Note: Because the student is being timed, it is important to pronounce any word not identified within three seconds. Quietly tell the student the word, have the student continue, and score the word as incorrect.

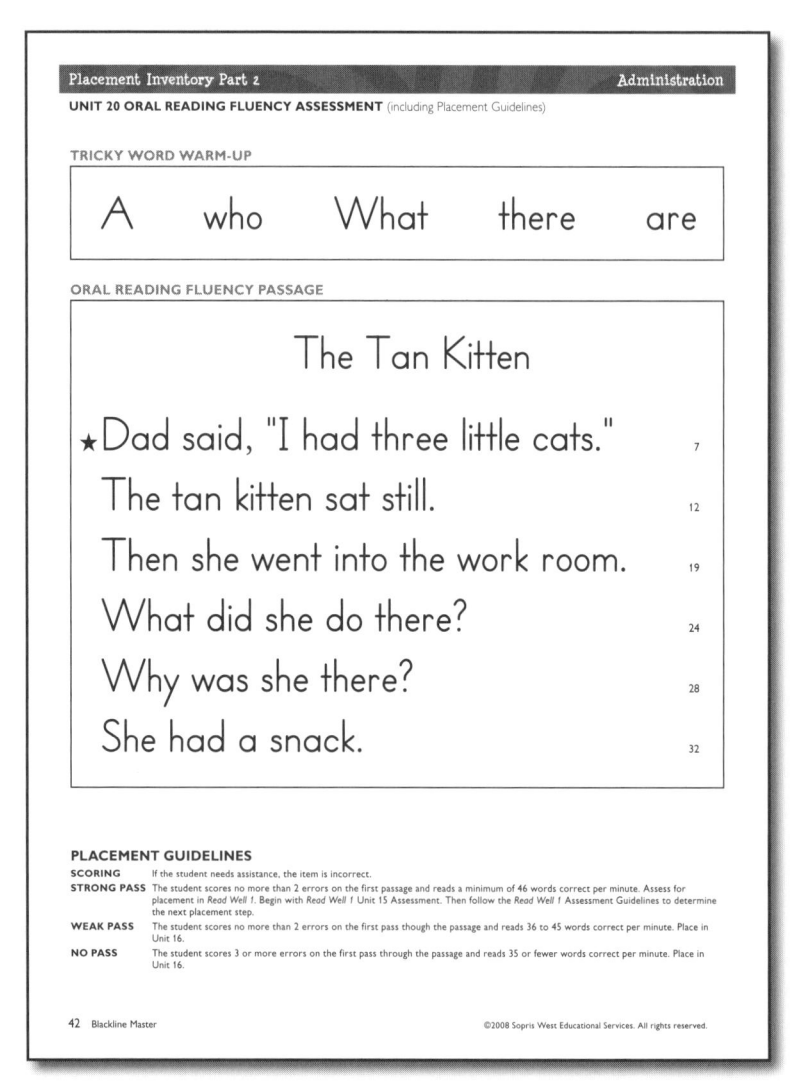

Placement Inventory Part 2 — Administration

UNIT 20 ORAL READING FLUENCY ASSESSMENT (including Placement Guidelines)

TRICKY WORD WARM-UP

A   who   What   there   are

ORAL READING FLUENCY PASSAGE

The Tan Kitten

★ Dad said, "I had three little cats." 7
The tan kitten sat still. 12
Then she went into the work room. 19
What did she do there? 24
Why was she there? 28
She had a snack. 32

PLACEMENT GUIDELINES

SCORING — If the student needs assistance, the item is incorrect.
STRONG PASS — The student scores no more than 2 errors on the first passage and reads a minimum of 46 words correct per minute. Assess for placement in *Read Well 1*. Begin with *Read Well 1* Unit 15 Assessment. Then follow the *Read Well 1* Assessment Guidelines to determine the next placement step.
WEAK PASS — The student scores no more than 2 errors on the first pass though the passage and reads 36 to 45 words correct per minute. Place in Unit 16.
NO PASS — The student scores 3 or more errors on the first pass through the passage and reads 35 or fewer words correct per minute. Place in Unit 16.

42 Blackline Master   ©2008 Sopris West Educational Services. All rights reserved.

Reproducible Placement Inventory Part 2, Unit 20 available on page 42.

SECTION 1 — Placement Administration

Placement Inventory Part 2

Juanita's Example

Student Placement Record Part 2

Name: Juanita R.   Teacher: Mr. Duncan

UNIT 20	ASSESSMENT ITEMS	SCORE/COMMENTS
Tricky Word Warm-Up	A who What there are	

Oral Reading Fluency Passage	The Tan Kitten
	★Dad said, "I had three little cats." 7
	    cat
	The tan kitten sat still. 12
	    SC
	Then she went (into) the (work) room. 19
	Why/What SC go
	What did she/do there? 24
	Why was she there? 28
	She had a snack. 32
		Accuracy: 3 Passage Errors
		
		Desired Fluency: 46+ words correct per minute
		Fluency: 51 WCPM
		(54 words read minus
		   3 errors in one minute)

Assessment Date(s):		SP (no more than 2 errors and 46 or more words correct per minute) WP (no more than 2 errors and 36 to 45 words correct per minute) (NP) (3 or more errors and/or 35 or fewer words correct per minute)

WCPM = words correct per minute

Strong Pass: Proceed to *Read Well 1*, Unit 15 Assessment.
Weak Pass or No Pass: Place in *Read Well K* Unit 16.

Reproducible Student Placement Record Part 2, Unit 20 available on page 46.

Student Placement Record, Part 1 and Part 2 Summary

Name: Juanita R.   Date: Fall Placement   Teacher: Mr. Duncan

PART 1

Name Writing Warm-Up: *Juanita Ruiz*

Record a *plus* for each correct response and a *minus* for each incorrect response. On each subtest, stop if the student makes five consecutive errors. Point to the remaining rows and ask the student if he or she knows any other letters, sounds, or words.

Subtest A — Letter Names: all + ... 26/26
Subtest B — Letter Sounds: all + ... 26/26

Add the scores for Subtests A and B. Stop if the student scores 16 or fewer. Place in Prelude A. Proceed to Subtest C and D if the student scores 17 or more. **52/52 Subtests A & B**

Subtest C — High-Frequency Words: I +, said +, the +, was +, is +, his +, as +, has +, with +, a +   **10/10**

Subtest D — Pattern Words: I'm +, see +, me +, am +, Dad +, seed +, than +, ant +, weed +, mint +, him +, can +   **12/12**

Add the scores for Subtests C and D. Stop if the student's combined score on Subtests A–D is 25 or fewer and place in Prelude A.
Proceed to Placement Inventory Part 2, Unit 1 Decoding Assessment if the student's total score is 26 or more.
22/22 Subtests C & D
74/74 Total Score A–D

PART 2 SUMMARY

Record a SP (Strong Pass), P (Pass), WP (Weak Pass), or NP (No Pass). Stop when the student scores a No Pass or a Weak Pass on any given assessment. Go back and place the student one unit higher than the last assessment with a Strong Pass.

Unit 1: P Pass (Administer Unit 5)   ___ No Pass (Place in Prelude A)
Unit 5: P Pass (Administer Unit 9)   ___ No Pass (Place in Unit 1)
Unit 9: SP Strong Pass (Administer Unit 15)   ___ Weak or No Pass (Place in Unit 6)
Unit 15: SP Strong Pass (Administer Unit 20)   ___ Weak or No Pass (Place in Unit 10)
Unit 20: ___ Strong Pass (Administer the *Read Well 1*, Unit 16 Assessment)   NP Weak or No Pass (Place in *RWK* Unit 16)

Reproducible Student Placement Record, Part 1 and Part 2 Summary available on page 43.

SECTION 1 Placement Administration

Summary of Placement Inventory

Placement Inventory Part 1

Administer the Placement Inventory Part 1 to all students.

SUBTEST A (LETTER NAMES) AND SUBTEST B (SOUNDS)	
If the student scores...	**Then...**
16 or fewer	Stop the assessment and place in Prelude A
17 or more	Continue with Subtests C and D

SUBTEST C (HIGH-FREQUENCY WORDS) AND SUBTEST D (PATTERN WORDS)	
If the student scores...	**Then...**
25 or fewer (total score) on Subtests A, B, C, and D	Stop the assessment and place in Prelude A
26 or more (total score) on Subtests A, B, C, and D	Continue with Part 2

Placement Inventory Part 2

ADMINISTRATION AND PLACEMENT SCHEDULE		
Administer test for...	**If the student scores a...**	**Then...**
Unit 1	No Pass / Pass	Place in Prelude A / Administer Unit 5
Unit 5	No Pass / Pass	Place in Unit 1 / Administer Unit 9
Unit 9	Weak or No Pass / Strong Pass	Place in Unit 6 / Administer Unit 15
Unit 15	Weak or No Pass / Strong Pass	Place in Unit 10 / Administer Unit 20
Unit 20	Weak or No Pass / Strong Pass	Place in Unit 16 / Administer the *Read Well 1*, Unit 16 Assessment

SECTION 1   Placement Administration

Placing Students

Preliminary Decisions

Once all students have been assessed, preliminary placements can be made.

- Determine whether you will group across grade levels, within grade levels, or only within your room.
- Determine how many groups you can teach. Each group will eventually need 30 minutes of instruction, ideally five days per week. Additional groups can be added when paraprofessionals are trained to assist with instruction and schoolwide schedules are designed to provide a well-staffed reading block.
- There will be a range of student skills within every group; however, the smaller the range, the better. Groups will vary in size. Some groups may be as large as eight students.

> **APPROPRIATE PLACEMENT OPTIONS**
>
> Collaboration is the key to providing every child with developmentally appropriate placement options *and* sufficient amounts of instructional time.

Grouping Students

1. Sort the students' Placement Inventory Records into sets according to where they place (Prelude A; Units 1, 6, 10, 16; and out-of-program).
2. Within each set, sort the Placement Inventory Records from high to low, based on the total scores for Part 1.
3. Make a copy of the Group Placement Form on page 47. Record student names by unit placement, and then by total scores from highest to lowest.
4. Using the ranked scores from the Group Placement Form, divide students into groups, based on the number of instructors available.
5. Determine where to begin instruction. For each group, begin at the lowest-scoring student's placement level. For example, if you have a group of six that includes four students who place in Unit 10 and two students who place in Unit 6, begin instruction in Unit 6. Arrange additional practice for the lowest-scoring students. Provide five minutes of instruction to the lowest two students before calling the remainder of the group. Set up cross-age tutoring or additional reading time with a parent volunteer.
6. Once instruction has begun, adjust groupings frequently to meet the needs of individual students.

> **CAUTION**
>
> Always place conservatively.
>
> Do not place a child higher than the Placement Inventory indicates.

SECTION 1 — Placement Administration
Placing Students

Lincoln School's Example—Kindergarten Collaboration

Lincoln School is located in a high-risk neighborhood. The staff at Lincoln has made a strong professional commitment to helping all children read well. Decisions regarding curricula are research based. Decisions about scheduling, staffing, and intervention are based on the knowledge that student success in a high-risk population rests in the hands of a coordinated staff effort. The staff is committed to the following:

- Use of *Read Well K* in kindergarten
- Use of *Read Well 1* and *Read Well Plus* in first grade
- Use of *Read Well 1* and *Read Well Plus* in second grade, as needed
- Use of *Read Well 1* and *Read Well Plus,* as needed for remediation in third grade
- Staff training and coaching in *Read Well*
- A one-hour, protected reading block for each grade level
- Scheduled time with Title I and special education staff during the reading block

Staffing and Scheduling Decisions

The hour from 9:00 A.M. to 10:00 A.M. is a scheduled, uninterrupted reading time for kindergarten. During this time, the classroom, Title I, and special education staff provide concentrated Small Group instruction. Each kindergarten classroom is staffed with an additional instructor during the reading block.

The kindergarten staff at Lincoln School has decided to teach their own reading groups for the first semester. During the second semester, students are regrouped across classrooms to increase the ability of teachers to provide developmentally appropriate instruction for all children.

Administering the Placement Inventory

The Title I teacher and paraprofessional, special education teacher, and two kindergarten paraprofessionals administer the Placement Inventory to all kindergarten students during the first few weeks of school. During this time, the classroom teachers provide Whole Class instruction in *Read Well K* Units 1, 2 and 3.

SECTION 1: Placement Administration
Placing Students

Results: Mrs. Jones' Kindergarten

Mrs. Jones is one of the three teachers at Lincoln. Mrs. Jones has a class of 25 kindergarten students. She has the assistance of a paraprofessional during the reading block. Mrs. Hollister works in Mrs. Jones' class for 60 minutes, five days each week.

Week 1
A school assessment team administers the Placement Inventory to all the students in the class. Mrs. Jones teaches *Read Well K* Whole Class Unit 1.

Weeks 2 and 3
Mrs. Jones teaches *Read Well K* Whole Class Units 2 and 3.

Week 4
Mrs. Jones is ready to begin Small Group instruction. Based on the Placement Inventory results and classroom observations, Mrs. Jones establishes four basic groups. Mrs. Jones and Mrs. Hollister will each teach two groups per day, rotating between groups every three weeks.

Explanation of Groupings

Mrs. Jones has one student, Dillon, who places in *Read Well K* at Unit 16. Mrs. Jones and Dillon's mother decide that Dillon can join a group of five students from other classrooms who will begin instruction at Unit 10. These students will work with a paraprofessional and the building reading specialist.

Group 1
Group 1 will begin instruction at Unit 1.

Group 2
Group 2 will begin instruction at Prelude A, moving at a regular pace. Students in this group demonstrated knowledge of most of the letter names and some letter sounds but were unable to pass the Unit 1 Placement Assessment. Mrs. Jones will try this group on a 6-Day Prelude A Plan. After giving the Prelude A Assessment, Mrs. Jones will determine whether the group will continue with Prelude A Extra Practice Lessons or move forward into Prelude B.

SECTION 1 Placement Administration
Placing Students

Group 3
Group 3 will begin instruction at Prelude A, moving at a moderate pace. Students in this group demonstrated knowledge of many of the letter names, but few or no letter sounds, and were unable to pass the Unit 1 Decoding Assessment. Mrs. Jones anticipates that this group will need an 8-Day Prelude A Plan.

Group 4
Group 4 will also begin instruction at Prelude A, moving at a slower pace. Students in this group demonstrated little or no knowledge of letter names and no knowledge of letter sounds. Mrs. Jones anticipates that this group will need a 10-Day Prelude A Plan.

Mrs. Jones will use cross-age tutors and parent volunteers whenever possible to provide these students with a second dose of reading.

Placement Inventory, Group Placement Form

DATE: Sept. 20   TEACHER(S): Mrs. Jones

STUDENT NAME	Group Placement	Possible In-Program Placement	Part 1 Total Score	Letter Names	Sounds	High-Frequency Words	Pattern Words	Comments
Dillon	Adv	Unit 16	73	26	12	19	16	*Walk to read with students from other classes.
Taylor	1	Unit 1	36	25	5	4	2	try 5-Day Plan
Hector	1	Unit 1	33	26	4	2	1	try 5-Day Plan
Miguel	1	Unit 1	29	25	3	0	0	try 5-Day Plan
Nick	1	Unit 1	28	24	3	1	1	try 5-Day Plan
Lydia	1	Unit 1	26	23	3	0	0	try 5-Day Plan
Naseem	1	Unit 1	26	23	3	0	0	try 5-Day Plan
Darius	1	Unit 1	24	20	4	0	0	try 5-Day Plan
Anthony	2	Prelude A	21	18	3	0	0	try 6-Day Plan
Mimi	2	Prelude A	21	19	2	0	1	try 6-Day Plan
Alma	2	Prelude A	19	17	3	0	0	try 6-Day Plan
Yolanda	2	Prelude A	18	15	3	0	0	try 6-Day Plan
Narou	2	Prelude A	17	14	3	0	0	try 6-Day Plan
Jake	3	Prelude A	16	13	3	0	1	8-Day Plan
Michael	3	Prelude A	15	13	2	0	0	8-Day Plan
Lee	3	Prelude A	15	12	3	0	0	8-Day Plan
Collin	3	Prelude A	15	12	3	0	0	8-Day Plan
Erik	3	Prelude A	11	9	2	0	0	8-Day Plan
Lisa	4	Prelude A	6	5	1	0	0	10-Day Plan, Double Dose
Nick	4	Prelude A	5	4	1	0	0	10-Day Plan, Double Dose
Emma	4	Prelude A	2	2	0	0	0	10-Day Plan, Double Dose
Bianca	4	Prelude A	1	1	0	0	0	10-Day Plan, Double Dose
Diego	4	Prelude A	0	0	0	0	0	10-Day Plan, Double Dose
James	4	Prelude A	0	0	0	0	0	10-Day Plan, Double Dose
Nadia	4	Prelude A	0	0	0	0	0	10-Day Plan, Double Dose

Reproducible Placement Inventory, Group Placement Form available on page 47.

SECTION 2

Placement Inventory and Forms

This section includes the Placement Inventory and record keeping forms.

Placement Inventory Part 1—Administration 34

Placement Inventory Part 2—Administration 37

Student Placement Records 43

Group Placement Form 47

Permission to reprint the Placement Inventory forms is provided on the copyright page of this manual.

Placement Inventory Part 1 — Administration

NAME WRITING WARM-UP

SUBTEST A. LETTER NAMES

A E H K M R

S W Z C D I

J N P T V Y

B F G L O Q

U X

Placement Inventory Part 1 — Administration

SUBTEST B. SOUNDS

s e m a d n

t w i h c r

k l o b g f

u y p v j qu

x z

Placement Inventory Part 1 — Administration

SUBTEST C. HIGH-FREQUENCY WORDS

I said the was is

his as has with a

SUBTEST D. PATTERN WORDS

I'm see me am

Dad seed than ant

weed mint him can

Placement Inventory Part 2 — Administration

UNIT 1 DECODING ASSESSMENT (including teacher's model on Subtest B and Placement Guidelines)

SUBTEST A. SOUNDS AND WORDS GOAL 6/6

S m a s M I

SUBTEST B. TEACHER'S MODEL, SMOOTH AND BUMPY BLENDING

m m m   mmm

SUBTEST B. SMOOTH AND BUMPY BLENDING GOAL 4/4

s s s   sss   a a a   aaa

SUBTEST C. FINGER TRACKING GOAL 4/4

s I S I

PLACEMENT GUIDELINES

SCORING If the student needs assistance, the item is incorrect.
PASS The student meets the goals on all subtests. Proceed to Unit 5 Placement Assessment.
NO PASS The student fails to meet the goals on 1 or more subtests. Place in Prelude A.

©2008 Sopris West Educational Services. All rights reserved.

| Placement Inventory Part 2 | Administration |

UNIT 5 DECODING ASSESSMENT (including teacher's model on Subtest B and Placement Guidelines)

SUBTEST A. SOUNDS GOAL 5/6

M   d   ee   s   a   D

SUBTEST B. TEACHER'S MODEL, SMOOTH AND BUMPY BLENDING

m e   me

SUBTEST B. SMOOTH AND BUMPY BLENDING GOAL 2/2

a m   am

SUBTEST C. SMOOTH BLENDING GOAL 3/4

Seed   me   add   dad

SUBTEST D. TRICKY WORDS GOAL 2/2

Said   I

(continued)

38 Blackline Master ©2008 Sopris West Educational Services. All rights reserved.

Placement Inventory Part 2　　　　　　　　　　　　　　　　　　　**Administration**

UNIT 5 DECODING ASSESSMENT *(continued)*

SUBTEST E. SENTENCES　　　　　　　　　　　　　　　　　　　　**GOAL 6/7**

"I'm sad.

I see me," said Dad.

PLACEMENT GUIDELINES
SCORING　　If the student needs assistance, the item is incorrect.
PASS　　　　The student meets the goals on all subtests. Proceed to Unit 9 Placement Assessment.
NO PASS　　The student fails to meet the goals on 1 or more subtests. Place in Unit 1.

Placement Inventory Part 2   **Administration**

UNIT 9 DECODING ASSESSMENT (including Placement Guidelines)

SUBTEST A. SOUNDS   GOAL 5/6

| a | t | ee | M | W | n |

SUBTEST B. SMOOTH BLENDING   GOAL 3/4

| we | sat | Than | Meet |

SUBTEST C. TRICKY WORDS   GOAL 3/3

| Said | the | was |

SUBTEST D. SENTENCES Desired Fluency: 20 seconds or less   GOAL 9/10

Dad said, "See the weeds."

We see that sad man.

PLACEMENT GUIDELINES

- **SCORING**   If the student needs assistance, the item is incorrect.
- **STRONG PASS**   The student meets the goals on all subtests and has attained the desired fluency. Proceed to Unit 15 Placement Assessment.
- **WEAK PASS**   The student meets the goals on 3 out of 4 subtests and/or fails to attain the desired fluency. Place in Unit 6.
- **NO PASS**   The student fails to meet the goals on 2 or more subtests and/or has not attained the desired fluency. Place in Unit 6.

Placement Inventory Part 2 **Administration**

UNIT 15 DECODING ASSESSMENT (including Placement Guidelines)

SUBTEST A. SOUNDS AND WORDS   GOAL 6/7

R   ck   i   ea   sh   a   K

SUBTEST B. SMOOTH BLENDING   GOAL 4/5

ink   Cass   mean   dish   can't

SUBTEST C. TRICKY WORDS   GOAL 4/5

should   his   a   wasn't   isn't

SUBTEST D. SENTENCES Desired Fluency: 30 seconds or less (34–36 WCPM)   GOAL 17/18

"Kim was sick that week," said Rick.

I wish she could kick.

"This isn't a trick," said Kim.

PLACEMENT GUIDELINES
SCORING   If the student needs assistance, the item is incorrect.
STRONG PASS   The student meets the goals on all subtests and has attained the desired fluency. Proceed to Unit 20.
WEAK PASS   The student meets the goals on 3 out of 4 subtests and/or fails to attain the desired fluency. Place in Unit 10.
NO PASS   The student fails to meet the goals on 2 or more subtests. Place in Unit 10.

©2008 Sopris West Educational Services. All rights reserved.

Placement Inventory Part 2 — Administration

UNIT 20 ORAL READING FLUENCY ASSESSMENT (including Placement Guidelines)

TRICKY WORD WARM-UP

A   who   What   there   are

ORAL READING FLUENCY PASSAGE

The Tan Kitten

★ Dad said, "I had three little cats."   7
The tan kitten sat still.   12
Then she went into the work room.   19
What did she do there?   24
Why was she there?   28
She had a snack.   32

PLACEMENT GUIDELINES

SCORING If the student needs assistance, the item is incorrect.

STRONG PASS The student scores no more than 2 errors on the first passage and reads a minimum of 46 words correct per minute. Assess for placement in *Read Well 1*. Begin with *Read Well 1* Unit 15 Assessment. Then follow the *Read Well 1* Assessment Guidelines to determine the next placement step.

WEAK PASS The student scores no more than 2 errors on the first pass though the passage and reads 36 to 45 words correct per minute. Place in Unit 16.

NO PASS The student scores 3 or more errors on the first pass through the passage and reads 35 or fewer words correct per minute. Place in Unit 16.

Student Placement Record, Part 1 and Part 2 Summary

Name _____ Date _____ Teacher _____

PART 1

Name Writing Warm-Up

Record a *plus* for each correct response and a *minus* for each incorrect response. On each subtest, stop if the student makes five consecutive errors. Point to the remaining rows and ask the student if he or she knows any other letters, sounds, or words.

Subtest A Letter Names	A ___ S ___ J ___ B ___ U ___	E ___ W ___ N ___ F ___ X ___	H ___ Z ___ P ___ G ___	K ___ C ___ T ___ L ___	M ___ D ___ V ___ O ___	R ___ I ___ Y ___ Q ___	___/26
Subtest B Letter Sounds	s ___ t ___ k ___ u ___ x ___	e ___ w ___ l ___ y ___ z ___	m ___ i ___ o ___ p ___	a ___ h ___ b ___ v ___	d ___ c ___ g ___ j ___	n ___ r ___ f ___ qu ___	___/26
	Add the scores for Subtests A and B. Stop if the student scores 16 or fewer. Place in Prelude A. Proceed to Subtest C and D if the student scores 17 or more.							___/52 Subtests A & B
Subtest C High-Frequency Words	I ___ said ___ the ___ was ___ is ___ his ___ as ___ has ___ with ___ a ___						___/10
Subtest D Pattern Words	I'm ___ see ___ me ___ am ___ Dad ___ seed ___ than ___ ant ___ weed ___ mint ___ him ___ can ___						___/12
	Add the scores for Subtests C and D. Stop if the student's combined score on Subtests A–D is 25 or fewer and place in Prelude A. Proceed to Placement Inventory Part 2, Unit 1 Decoding Assessment if the student's total score is 26 or more.							___/22 Subtests C & D ___/74 Total Score A–D

PART 2 SUMMARY

Record a SP (Strong Pass), P (Pass), WP (Weak Pass), or NP (No Pass). Stop when the student scores a No Pass or a Weak Pass on any given assessment. Go back and place the student one unit higher than the last assessment with a Strong Pass.

Unit 1:	_____ Pass (Administer Unit 5)	_____ No Pass (Place in Prelude A)
Unit 5:	_____ Pass (Administer Unit 9)	_____ No Pass (Place in Unit 1)
Unit 9:	_____ Strong Pass (Administer Unit 15)	_____ Weak or No Pass (Place in Unit 6)
Unit 15:	_____ Strong Pass (Administer Unit 20)	_____ Weak or No Pass (Place in Unit 10)
Unit 20:	_____ Strong Pass (Administer the *Read Well 1*, Unit 16 Assessment)	_____ Weak or No Pass (Place in *RWK* Unit 16)

©2008 Sopris West Educational Services. All rights reserved.

Blackline Master 43

Student Placement Record Part 2

Name _____ Teacher _____

IMPORTANT: Follow the scoring and recording procedures shown on pages 16 and 23. For each unit, circle the student's pass level appropriately: SP (Strong Pass), P (Pass), WP (Weak Pass), NP (No Pass).

Note: Before administering Subtest B on Units 1 and 5 Decoding Assessments, demonstrate how to do Smooth and Bumpy Blending, using the models provided on the Administration pages.

UNIT 1	ASSESSMENT ITEMS	SCORE/COMMENTS
Subtest A	S m a s M I	Goal 6/6 ____/6
Subtest B	s·s·s sss a·a·a aaa	Goal 4/4 ____/4
Subtest C	S̩ I̩ S̩ I̩	Goal 4/4 ____/4
Assessment Date(s):		Goals Met ____/3 Subtests P (all subtests) NP

Pass: Proceed to Unit 5 Assessment.
No Pass: Place in Prelude A.

UNIT 5	ASSESSMENT ITEMS	SCORE/COMMENTS
Subtest A	M d ee s a D	Goal 5/6 ____/6
Subtest B	a·m am	Goal 2/2 ____/2
Subtest C	Seed me add dad	Goal 3/4 ____/4
Subtest D	Said I	Goal 2/2 ____/2
Subtest E	"I'm sad. I see me," said Dad.	Goal 6/7 ____/7
Assessment Date(s):		Goals Met ____/5 Subtests P (all subtests) NP

Pass: Proceed to Unit 9 Assessment.
No Pass: Place in Unit 1.

44 Blackline Master ©2008 Sopris West Educational Services. All rights reserved.

Student Placement Record Part 2

Name _____ Teacher _____

UNIT 9	ASSESSMENT ITEMS	SCORE/COMMENTS
Subtest A	a t ee M W n	Goal 5/6 ____/6
Subtest B	we sat Than Meet	Goal 3/4 ____/4
Subtest C	Said the was	Goal 3/3 ____/3
Subtest D	Dad said, "See the weeds." We see that sad man.	Accuracy Goal 9/10 ____/10 words correct Desired Fluency: 20 seconds or less (10/20 in 20 seconds = 30 WCPM) ____ seconds
Assessment Date(s):		Goals Met ____/4 Subtests SP (all subtests with desired fluency) WP (3/4 subtests and/or fails to attain the desired fluency) NP (fails two or more subtests)

Strong Pass: Proceed to Unit 15 Assessment.
Weak Pass or No Pass: Place in Unit 6.

UNIT 15	ASSESSMENT ITEMS	SCORE/COMMENTS
Subtest A	R ck i ea sh a K	Goal 6/7 ____/7
Subtest B	ink Cass mean dish can't	Goal 4/5 ____/5
Subtest C	should his a wasn't isn't	Goal 4/5 ____/5
Subtest D	"Kim was sick that week," said Rick. I wish she could kick. "This isn't a trick," said Kim.	Accuracy Goal 17/18 ____/18 words correct Desired Fluency: 30 seconds or less (18/18 in 30 seconds = 36 WCPM) ____ seconds
Assessment Date(s):		Goals Met ____/4 Subtests SP (all subtests with desired fluency) WP (3/4 subtests and/or fails to attain the desired fluency) NP (fails two or more subtests)

Strong Pass: Proceed to Unit 20 Assessment.
Weak Pass or No Pass: Place in Unit 10.

WCPM = words correct per minute

©2008 Sopris West Educational Services. All rights reserved.

Student Placement Record Part 2

Name _____ Teacher _____

UNIT 20	ASSESSMENT ITEMS	SCORE/COMMENTS
Tricky Word Warm-Up	A who What there are	
Oral Reading Fluency Passage	The Tan Kitten ★Dad said, "I had three little cats." 7 The tan kitten sat still. 12 Then she went into the work room. 19 What did she do there? 24 Why was she there? 28 She had a snack. 32	**Accuracy:** ____ Passage Errors Desired Fluency: 46+ words correct per minute **Fluency:** ____ WCPM (____ words read minus ____ errors in one minute)
Assessment Date(s):	SP (no more than 2 errors and 46 or more words correct per minute) WP (no more than 2 errors and 36 to 45 words correct per minute) NP (3 or more errors and/or 35 or fewer words correct per minute)	

WCPM = words correct per minute

Strong Pass: Proceed to *Read Well 1*, Unit 15 Assessment.
Weak Pass or No Pass: Place in *Read Well K* Unit 16.

46 Blackline Master   ©2008 Sopris West Educational Services. All rights reserved.

Placement Inventory, Group Placement Form

DATE _____ TEACHER(S) _____

STUDENT NAME	Group Placement	Possible In-Program Placement	Part 1 Total Score	Letter Names	Sounds	High-Frequency Words	Pattern Words	Comments

SECTION 3
Ongoing Assessment

This section explains how to use end-of-the unit assessments to maximize progress for each child as he or she moves through the program.

Overview 49

Managing Assessments 51

Decoding Assessments, Preludes–Unit 15 54

Oral Reading Fluency Assessments, Units 16–20 62

Decoding Diagnosis, Unit 20 66

SECTION 3 Ongoing Assessment

Overview

Young children thrive when their lessons are supportive and successful. Because each child is unique in his or her background knowledge, response to instruction, and predisposition to reading, it is critical to deliver lessons that are tailored to the needs of each child.

At the end of each Prelude and unit, you will quickly assess each child's progress. *Read Well* Assessments will help you determine whether a child is ready to learn new skills or would benefit from:

- Additional lessons in a unit
- A quick review to firm up past learning
- A slower pace of instruction
- A faster pace of instruction
- Instruction in a different group.

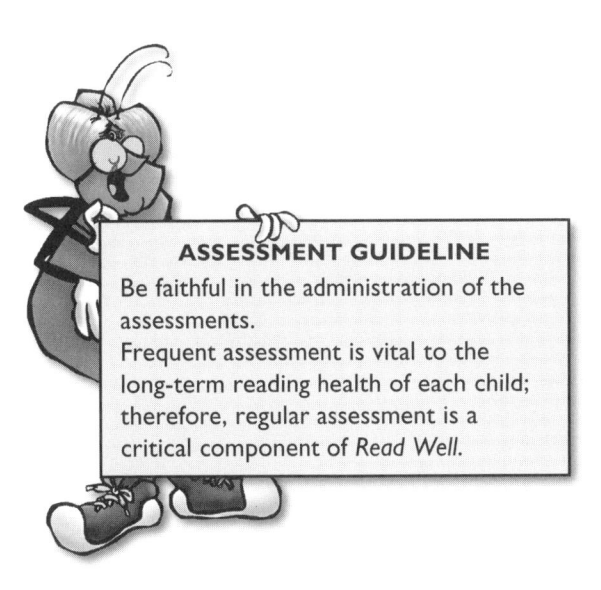

ASSESSMENT GUIDELINE
Be faithful in the administration of the assessments.
Frequent assessment is vital to the long-term reading health of each child; therefore, regular assessment is a critical component of *Read Well*.

SECTION 3 Ongoing Assessment

What Is Assessed

Because assessment can cut into instructional time, *Read Well K* Assessments were designed to quickly measure student mastery of newly introduced skills and to monitor maintenance of previously learned skills. Less frequent but more comprehensive assessment is advisable at the beginning, middle, and end of each school year.

Decoding Assessments—Preludes A, B, C
These assessments evaluate:

- Knowledge of sounds
- Knowledge of everyday picture words
- Comprehension (Who is the story about? What is (s)he doing?)

Decoding Assessments—Units 1–15
These assessments evaluate:

- Knowledge of sounds
- Ability to blend sounds smoothly
- Ability to blend sounds smoothly into words
- Knowledge of Tricky Words (words that do not sound out based on sounds taught)
- Sentence reading and fluency

    (If you wish to do additional monitoring of comprehension, each unit storybook includes a Story Summary that can be used as a retell activity.)

Oral Reading Fluency Assessments—Units 16–20
These assessments evaluate:

- Knowledge of recently introduced Tricky Words (irregular words)
- Oral reading fluency (words correct per minute)

Note: Fluency scores also provide you with information about the range of performance in a group, indicating which students need more practice.

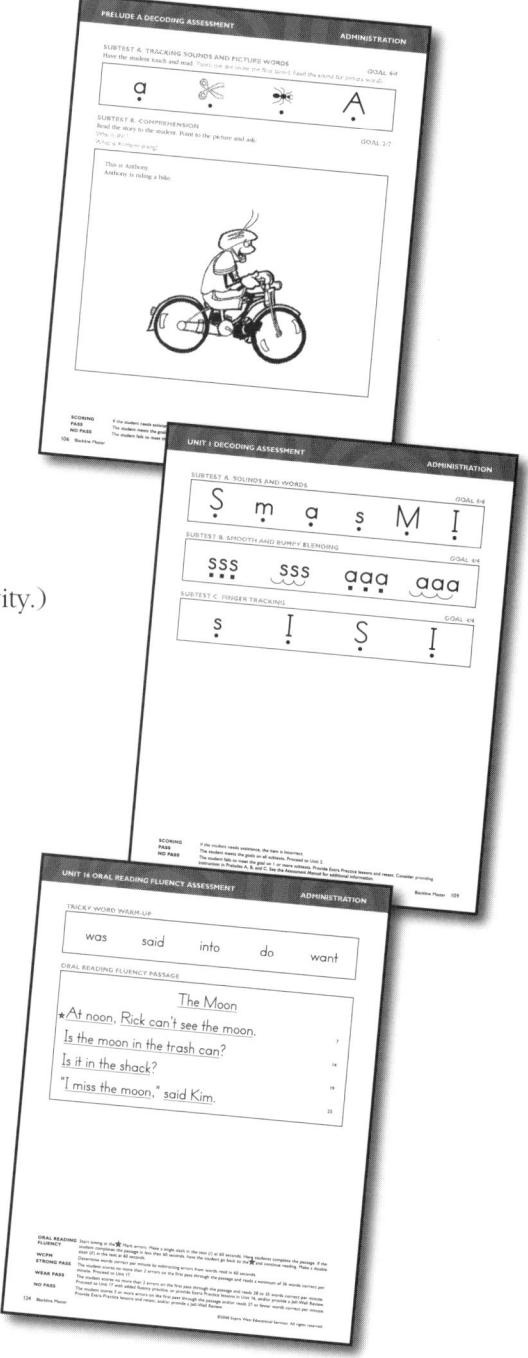

SECTION 3 Ongoing Assessment

Managing Assessments

Who Administers the Assessments

Most instructors assess the groups they teach. However, other trained professionals (e.g., instructional assistants, specialists, and other teachers) can assess individuals and should periodically assess groups to ensure consistency and objectivity.

When Assessments Are Administered

Read Well K Assessments are administered during an assessment lesson, at the end of each Prelude, and at the end of each unit. Progress is monitored frequently to prevent any child from becoming overwhelmed by the learning process and to keep pace with the developmental shifts that young children experience.

Because most teachers need to give assessments during group time, assessment lessons are shorter and include independent activities for the other children to work on while you complete the one-to-one assessments. Assessment time ranges from 30 seconds to a few minutes per child. Assessments take longer as the children move through the program.

1. Prelude instruction includes an assessment lesson on:
   - Day 6 of a 6-Day Plan
   - Day 7 of a 7-Day Plan
   - Day 8 of a 8-Day Plan
   - Day 9 of a 9-Day Plan
   - Day 10 of a 10-Day Plan

2. Units 1–20 include an assessment lesson on:
   - Day 5 of a 5-Day Plan
   - Day 7 of a 7-Day Plan
   - Day 9 of a 9-Day Plan
   - Day 12 of a 12-Day Plan

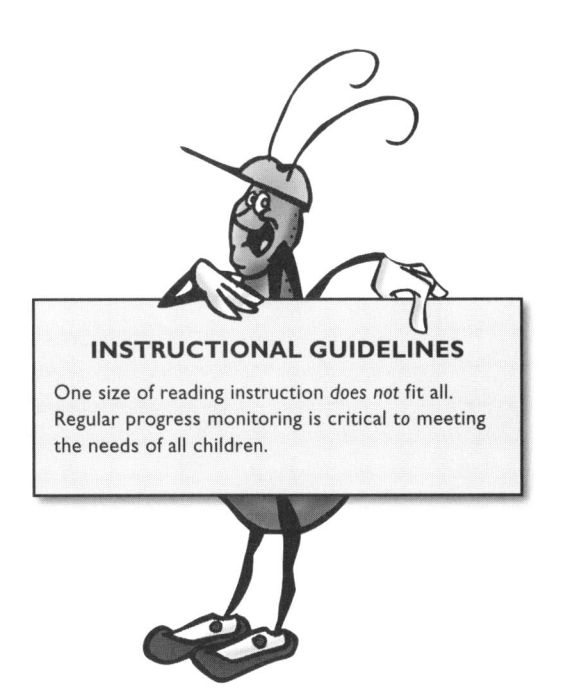

INSTRUCTIONAL GUIDELINES

One size of reading instruction *does not* fit all. Regular progress monitoring is critical to meeting the needs of all children.

SECTION 3 Ongoing Assessment
Managing Assessments

Materials Preparation

1. Make one copy per student of the Student Assessment Record (pages 130–141). This form is used to record and score student responses. (You may wish to organize Student Assessment Records in a Small Group folder or notebook.)

2. Make one copy per group of the Group Assessment Record.

3. Each person who will administer the assessments should be trained to administer and score the assessments.

4. Assessment Administration Forms are located in this manual (pages 106–129) and also at the end of each Prelude and unit teacher's guide.

5. Obtain stopwatches. The assessments for Units 6–20 include timings that measure students' oral reading fluency.

SECTION 3 — Ongoing Assessment
Managing Assessments

General Administration Guidelines

- Assess each student individually, where others cannot hear.
- Place the assessment on the desk so that the child can easily point to sounds and words.
- The student should not be able to see you score.
- Help the child feel comfortable. Most young children enjoy one-to-one time with an adult. Say something like:

    I'm glad I get to listen to you read today.

- Throughout the assessment, compliment the student on the things he or she can do.

    You know all the sounds we've practiced. I'm very proud of you.

- Score student responses on the Student Assessment Record, adhering to the scoring criteria on page 54.
- As appropriate, record a Strong Pass, Pass, Weak Pass, or No Pass.

SECTION 3 Ongoing Assessment

Decoding Assessments, Preludes–Unit 15

Preludes A–C and Units 1–15 are accompanied by assessments that provide information about skills. Scoring is done directly on each student's Student Assessment Record. Record responses using the diagnostic scoring explained and shown below. When the assessment is complete, circle Strong Pass, Pass, Weak Pass, or No Pass, as appropriate.

DIAGNOSTIC SCORING

If the student …	Record …
Needs Assistance Wait three seconds. Gently tell the student the correct response, draw a line through the item, and write an "A" for "assisted." Score as an incorrect response.	Incorrect She ~~should~~ swim in the sea. (A above should)
Mispronunciation Gently tell the student the correct response. Draw a line through the item and write the substituted word or sound. Score as an incorrect response.	Incorrect would with ~~wasn't~~ (was above wasn't)
Fails to Blend Smoothly Remind the student to do Smooth Blending, not Bumpy Blending. If the student still fails to blend smoothly (e.g., pauses or stops between sounds), guide Smooth Blending of the word. Draw a line through the item. Rewrite the word, drawing dashes between sounds to indicate where the student paused. Score as an incorrect response.	Incorrect she ~~Tad~~ can dash (T-ad above Tad)
Self-Corrects If the student spontaneously self-corrects, write "SC," so that you do not count the error. If the student requires more than two attempts, score as an incorrect response.	Correct I wish we could eat seeds. (SC above could)

TIMED SUBTEST

Sentences, Units 6–15

- As the student begins reading, start the stopwatch or note where the second hand is on your watch or clock.
- When the student completes Sentence Reading, record how many seconds to completion. If a student cannot read a word within three seconds, pronounce the word, score as incorrect, and encourage the student to keep reading.

SECTION 3 — Ongoing Assessment
Managing Assessments

Sample Student Assessment Record, Preludes A–C

Scoring is done directly on each individual student's Student Assessment Record. When the assessment is completed, circle Strong Pass, Pass, Weak Pass, or No Pass, as appropriate.

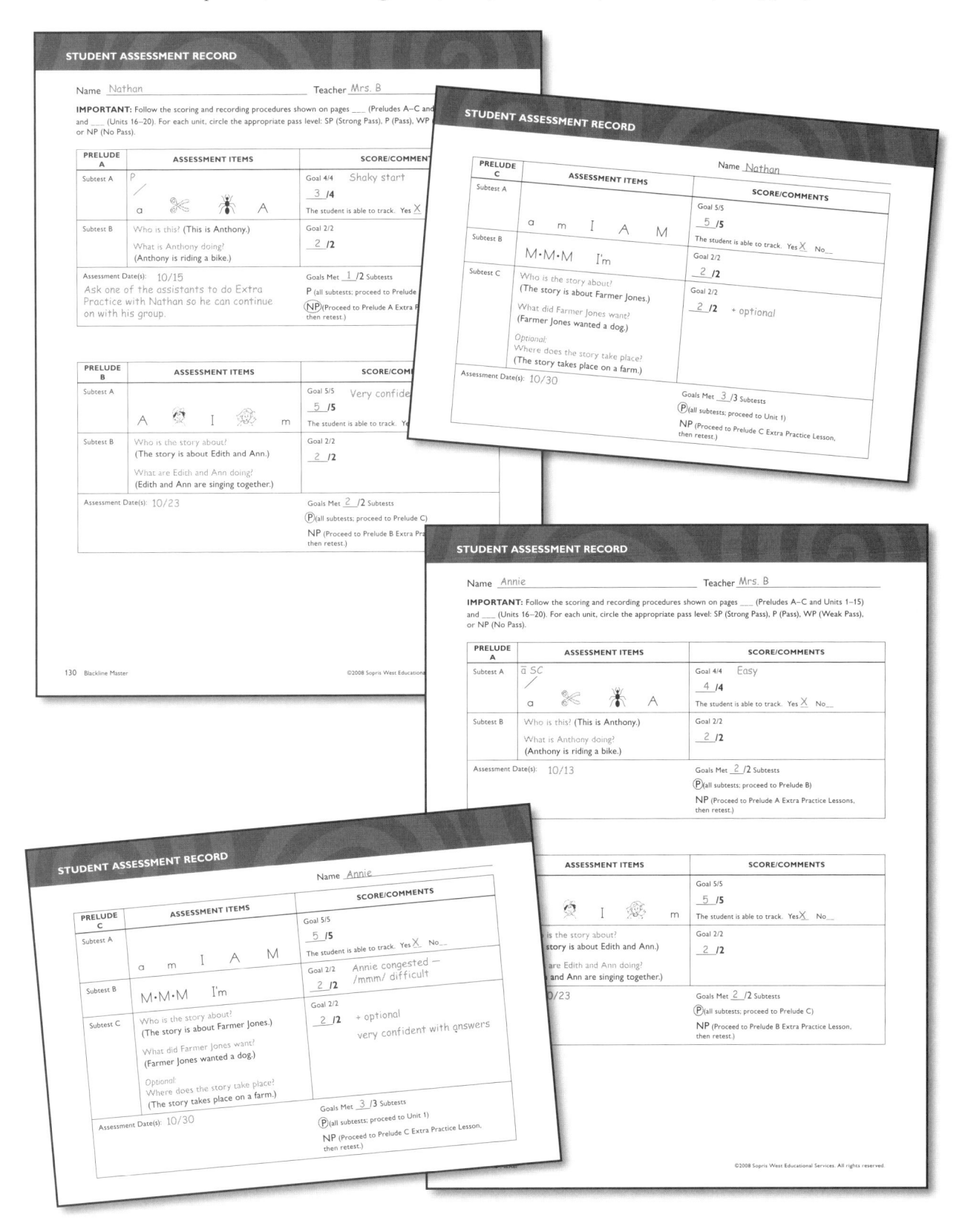

STUDENT ASSESSMENT RECORD

Name: Nathan   Teacher: Mrs. B

IMPORTANT: Follow the scoring and recording procedures shown on pages ___ (Preludes A–C and ___ (Units 16–20). For each unit, circle the appropriate pass level: SP (Strong Pass), P (Pass), WP (Weak Pass), or NP (No Pass).

PRELUDE A	ASSESSMENT ITEMS	SCORE/COMMENTS
Subtest A	P / a ✂ 🐜 A	Goal 4/4 Shaky start 3/4 The student is able to track. Yes X No __
Subtest B	Who is this? (This is Anthony.) What is Anthony doing? (Anthony is riding a bike.)	Goal 2/2 2/2
Assessment Date(s): 10/15 Ask one of the assistants to do Extra Practice with Nathan so he can continue on with his group.		Goals Met 1/2 Subtests P (all subtests; proceed to Prelude B) (NP) (Proceed to Prelude A Extra Practice Lessons, then retest.)

PRELUDE B	ASSESSMENT ITEMS	SCORE/COMMENTS
Subtest A	A 🐝 I 👧 m	Goal 5/5 Very confident 5/5 The student is able to track. Yes __
Subtest B	Who is the story about? (The story is about Edith and Ann.) What are Edith and Ann doing? (Edith and Ann are singing together.)	Goal 2/2 2/2
Assessment Date(s): 10/23		Goals Met 2/2 Subtests P (all subtests; proceed to Prelude C) NP (Proceed to Prelude B Extra Practice Lesson, then retest.)

130 Blackline Master   ©2008 Sopris West Educational Services

---

STUDENT ASSESSMENT RECORD

Name: Nathan

PRELUDE C	ASSESSMENT ITEMS	SCORE/COMMENTS
Subtest A	a m I A M	Goal 5/5 5/5 The student is able to track. Yes X No __
Subtest B	M·M·M I'm	Goal 2/2 2/2
Subtest C	Who is the story about? (The story is about Farmer Jones.) What did Farmer Jones want? (Farmer Jones wanted a dog.) Optional: Where does the story take place? (The story takes place on a farm.)	Goal 2/2 2/2 + optional
Assessment Date(s): 10/30		Goals Met 3/3 Subtests (P) (all subtests; proceed to Unit 1) NP (Proceed to Prelude C Extra Practice Lesson, then retest.)

STUDENT ASSESSMENT RECORD

Name: Annie   Teacher: Mrs. B

IMPORTANT: Follow the scoring and recording procedures shown on pages ___ (Preludes A–C and Units 1–15) and ___ (Units 16–20). For each unit, circle the appropriate pass level: SP (Strong Pass), P (Pass), WP (Weak Pass), or NP (No Pass).

PRELUDE A	ASSESSMENT ITEMS	SCORE/COMMENTS
Subtest A	ā SC / a ✂ 🐜 A	Goal 4/4 Easy 4/4 The student is able to track. Yes X No __
Subtest B	Who is this? (This is Anthony.) What is Anthony doing? (Anthony is riding a bike.)	Goal 2/2 2/2
Assessment Date(s): 10/13		Goals Met 2/2 Subtests (P) (all subtests; proceed to Prelude B) NP (Proceed to Prelude A Extra Practice Lessons, then retest.)

	ASSESSMENT ITEMS	SCORE/COMMENTS
	🐝 I 👧 m	Goal 5/5 5/5 The student is able to track. Yes X No __
	is the story about? story is about Edith and Ann.) are Edith and Ann doing? and Ann are singing together.)	Goal 2/2 2/2
10/23		Goals Met 2/2 Subtests (P) (all subtests; proceed to Prelude C) NP (Proceed to Prelude B Extra Practice Lesson, then retest.)

STUDENT ASSESSMENT RECORD

Name: Annie

PRELUDE C	ASSESSMENT ITEMS	SCORE/COMMENTS
Subtest A	a m I A M	Goal 5/5 5/5 The student is able to track. Yes X No __
Subtest B	M·M·M I'm	Goal 2/2 Annie congested — 2/2 /mmm/ difficult
Subtest C	Who is the story about? (The story is about Farmer Jones.) What did Farmer Jones want? (Farmer Jones wanted a dog.) Optional: Where does the story take place? (The story takes place on a farm.)	Goal 2/2 2/2 + optional very confident with answers
Assessment Date(s): 10/30		Goals Met 3/3 Subtests (P) (all subtests; proceed to Unit 1) NP (Proceed to Prelude C Extra Practice Lesson, then retest.)

©2008 Sopris West Educational Services. All rights reserved.

55

SECTION 3 — Ongoing Assessment
Managing Assessments

How to Administer Preludes A–C

While administering assessments, use each individual's Student Assessment Record to mark errors. The following is a sample of script for Prelude C.

Subtest A. Tracking Sounds and Picture Words

Tell the student to point to each item and say the picture word, word, or sound. Say something like:

Touch the dot under the first sound. Read the sound. (/ăăă/)

Touch the dot under the next picture word. Read the sound. (/mmm/)

Repeat with "I," /ăăă/, and /mmm/.

Subtest B. Smooth and Bumpy Blending

Have the student touch each square and do Bumpy Blending.

You get to do Bumpy Blending.

Touch the square under the first sound and do Bumpy Blending. (/m/•/m/•/m/)

Have the student follow the loop and do Smooth Blending.

Now do Smooth Blending. Put your finger at the beginning of the first loop and do Smooth Blending. (/lllmmm/)

Subtest C. Comprehension

Read the story to the student.

Ask the comprehension question found on the assessment.

Accept any reasonable response.

At the bottom of each assessment are general diagnostic prescriptions to help determine whether to teach the unit Extra Practice lessons or to move forward. (See pages 71–74 for additional information.)

PROVIDING ASSISTANCE

When giving an assessment, if you find yourself helping a student, score the item as incorrect. Your assistance means the student hasn't yet mastered the skill. Follow the prescriptions at the bottom of the assessment.

SECTION 3 — Ongoing Assessment
Managing Assessments

Sample: Prelude C Decoding Assessment

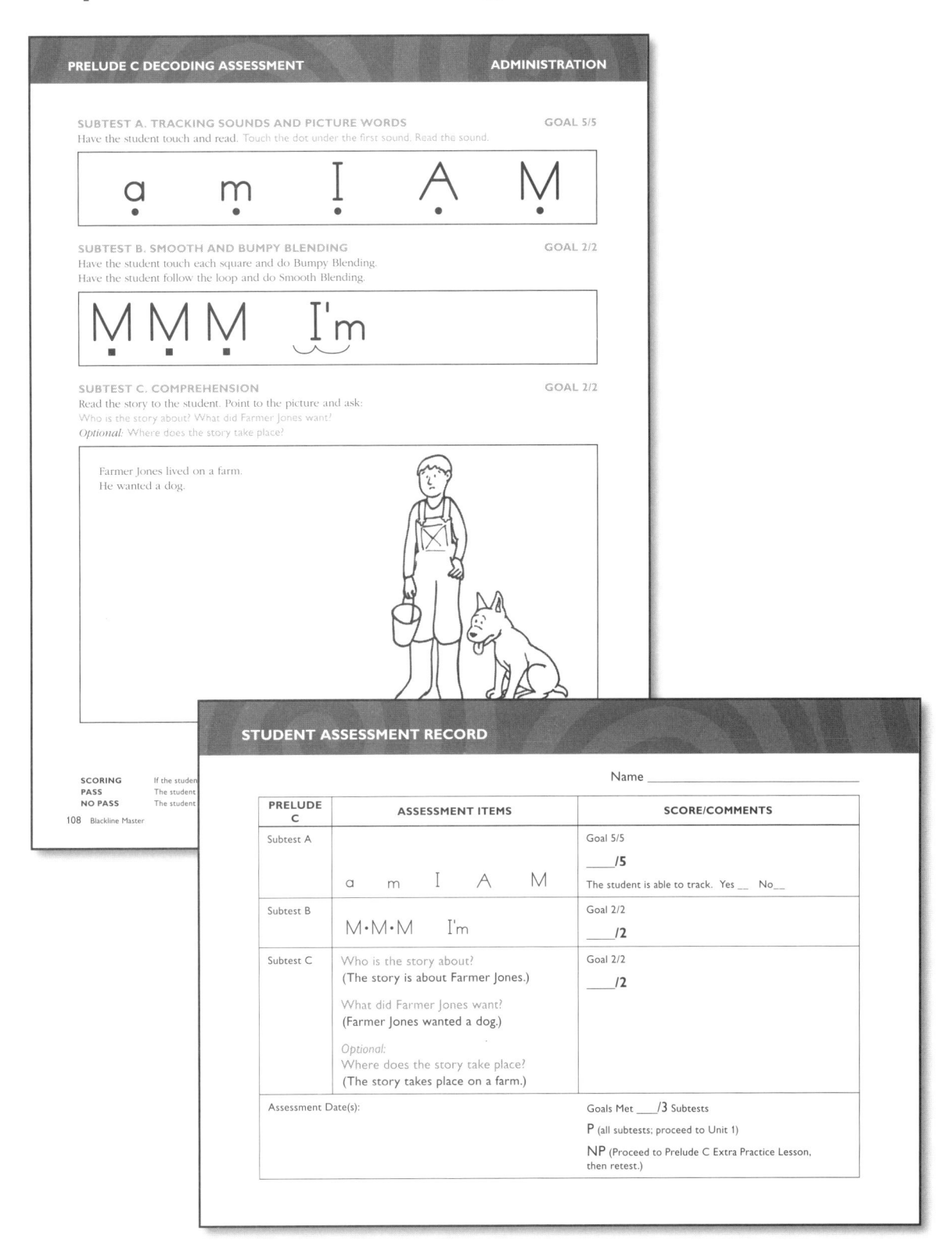

PRELUDE C DECODING ASSESSMENT — **ADMINISTRATION**

SUBTEST A. TRACKING SOUNDS AND PICTURE WORDS — GOAL 5/5
Have the student touch and read. Touch the dot under the first sound. Read the sound.

a   m   I   A   M

SUBTEST B. SMOOTH AND BUMPY BLENDING — GOAL 2/2
Have the student touch each square and do Bumpy Blending.
Have the student follow the loop and do Smooth Blending.

M M M   I'm

SUBTEST C. COMPREHENSION — GOAL 2/2
Read the story to the student. Point to the picture and ask:
Who is the story about? What did Farmer Jones want?
Optional: Where does the story take place?

Farmer Jones lived on a farm.
He wanted a dog.

SCORING — If the student...
PASS — The student...
NO PASS — The student...

108 Blackline Master

STUDENT ASSESSMENT RECORD

Name _____

PRELUDE C	ASSESSMENT ITEMS	SCORE/COMMENTS
Subtest A	a m I A M	Goal 5/5 ____/5 The student is able to track. Yes ___ No___
Subtest B	M·M·M I'm	Goal 2/2 ____/2
Subtest C	Who is the story about? (The story is about Farmer Jones.) What did Farmer Jones want? (Farmer Jones wanted a dog.) *Optional:* Where does the story take place? (The story takes place on a farm.)	Goal 2/2 ____/2
Assessment Date(s):		Goals Met ____/3 Subtests P (all subtests; proceed to Unit 1) NP (Proceed to Prelude C Extra Practice Lesson, then retest.)

57

SECTION 3 Ongoing Assessment
Managing Assessments

How to Administer Units 1–5

The Decoding Assessments for these units vary slightly. Unit 5 includes all five subtests. While administering assessments, use each individual's Student Assessment Record to mark errors. Following are sample scripts for Unit 5.

Subtest A. Sounds

Have the student point to each item and say the sound.
> Touch the dot under the first sound. Read the sound. (/mmm/)
> Read the next sound. (/d/)

Repeat with the remaining sounds.

Subtest B. Smooth and Bumpy Blending

Have the student touch each square and do Bumpy Blending.
> You get to do Bumpy Blending.
> Touch the square under the first sound and do Bumpy Blending. (/ă/•/m/)

Have the student follow the loops and do Smooth Blending.
> Now do Smooth Blending. Put your finger at the beginning of the first loop and do Smooth Blending. (/ăăămmm/)

Subtest C. Smooth Blending

Have the student do Smooth Blending of each word and then say the word.
> Do Smooth Blending. (/sssēēēd/)
> Say the word. (Seed)

Repeat with the remaining words.

Subtest D. Tricky Words

Have the student identify each Tricky Word.
> Put your finger under the first Tricky Word and read the word. (Said)
> Repeat with the remaining word.

Subtest E. Sentences

Have the student point to the first word and then read the sentence.
> You get to read sentences.
> Put your finger under the first word and start when you're ready. (I'm sad.)
> Keep reading. ("I see me," said Dad.)

General prescriptions are located at the bottom of each assessment.

SECTION 3 — Ongoing Assessment
Managing Assessments

Sample: Unit 5 Decoding Assessment

UNIT 5 DECODING ASSESSMENT — ADMINISTRATION

SUBTEST A. SOUNDS — GOAL 5/6

M d ee s a D

SUBTEST B. SMOOTH AND BUMPY BLENDING — GOAL 2/2

a m   am

SUBTEST C. SMOOTH BLENDING — GOAL 3/4

Seed me add dad

SUBTEST D. TRICKY WORDS — GOAL 2/2

Said I

SUBTEST E. SENTENCES — GOAL 6/7

"I'm sad.

I see me," said Dad.

SCORING
PASS
NO PASS

©2008 Sopris West Educational Services

STUDENT ASSESSMENT RECORD

Name: Solang

UNIT 5	ASSESSMENT ITEMS	SCORE/COMMENTS
Subtest A	M d ee s a D	Goal 5/6 6/6
Subtest B	a·m am	Goal 2/2 2/2
Subtest C	Seed me add ~~dad~~ d-ad	Goal 3/4 3/4
Subtest D	Said I	Goal 2/2 2/2
Subtest E	"I'm sad. I see me," said D-ad ~~Dad~~	Goal 6/7 6/7 Place "Dad" word card on Solang's desk. Practice Smooth and Bumpy Blending to mastery.
Assessment Date(s):		Goals Met 5/5 Subtests (P) (all subtests) NP

SECTION 3 Ongoing Assessment
Managing Assessments

How to Administer Units 6–15

Units 6–8 continue assessing Smooth and Bumpy Blending. At Unit 9, this subtest is dropped. Beginning with Unit 6, each assessment includes a timing of the sentences.

While administering assessments, use each individual's Student Assessment Record to mark errors and record the number of seconds required to read the sentences. Following are sample scripts for Unit 14.

Subtest A. Sounds

Have the student point to each item and say the sound.

Touch the dot under the first sound. Read the sound. (/k/)

Read the next sound. (/h/)

Repeat with the remaining sounds.

Subtest B. Smooth Blending

Have the student do Smooth Blending of each word and then say the word.

I know you can read some of these words very quickly, but I want to see if you can still do Smooth Blending. So I'm going to have you strrreeetch each word out.

Put your finger under the first word and do Smooth Blending. (/shshshēēē/)

Say the word. (she)

Repeat with the remaining words.

Subtest C. Tricky Words

Have the student identify each Tricky Word.

Put your finger under the first Tricky Word and read the word. (would)

Repeat with the remaining words.

Subtest D. Sentences

Have the student point to the first word and then read the sentence. Record the number of seconds to completion. (If a student is unable to read a word in 3 seconds, quickly tell the word and score as incorrect.)

You get to read sentences.

Put your finger under the first word and start when you're ready.
(She should swim in the . . .)

General prescriptions are located at the bottom of each assessment.

SECTION 3 — Ongoing Assessment
Managing Assessments

Sample: Unit 14 Decoding Assessment

UNIT 14 DECODING ASSESSMENT — ADMINISTRATION

SUBTEST A. SOUNDS — GOAL 6/7

c   H   e   r   i   w   Sh

SUBTEST B. SMOOTH BLENDING — GOAL 4/5

she   Tad   can   dash   read

SUBTEST C. TRICKY WORDS — GOAL 3/4

would   with   Want   wasn't

SUBTEST D. SENTENCES   Desired Fluency: 30 seconds or less (30–32 WCPM)   GOAL 15/16

She should swim in the sea.
I wish we could eat seeds
with Dean and Sam.

SCORING
STRONG PASS
WEAK PASS
NO PASS

122 Blackline Master

UNIT 14	ASSESSMENT ITEMS	SCORE/COMMENTS
Subtest A	c H e r i w Sh	Goal 6/7 _7_ /7
Subtest B	she Tad (T-ad) can dash read	Goal 4/5 _4_ /5
Subtest C	would with Want (went) wasn't	Goal 3/4 _3_ /4
Subtest D	She should swim in the sea. I wish we could eat seeds with Dean (D-ean SC) and Sam.	Accuracy Goal 15/16 _16_ /16 words correct Desired Fluency: 30 seconds or less (30–32 WCPM) _43_ seconds Have Cynthia do repeated readings with Parent Volunteers. (Solo Stories, Units 5–14)
Assessment Date(s): 3/15		Goals Met _4_ /4 Subtests SP (all subtests with desired fluency) (WP) (3/4 subtests, and/or fails to attain the desired fluency) NP (fails 2 or more subtests)

138 Blackline Master ©2008 Sopris West Educational Services. All rights reserved.

SECTION 3 Ongoing Assessment

Oral Reading Fluency Assessments, Units 16–20

Tricky Word Warm-Up

Have the student point to and read each word. Mark errors on the Student Assessment Record.

Oral Reading Fluency Passage

Passing criteria include two measures for the *same* passage reading.

- **Accuracy:** Number of errors made for the entire passage on the first time through
- **Oral Reading Fluency:** Words correct per minute (WCPM)—words read in one minute, minus the errors made in one minute (a measure of accuracy and speed).

Procedures

1. Have the student read the title of the passage and predict what the passage will be about.

2. Have the student point to the first word in the passage and track the text while reading the entire passage. Concurrently, time the reading.

    - Make a slash (/) in the text where the student is at 60 seconds (but have the student complete the passage).
    - If the student completes the passage in less than 60 seconds, have the student return to the ★ and continue reading until 60 seconds have passed. Use a double slash (//) to mark where the student is at 60 seconds.
    - As the student reads, code any errors using the scoring procedures on page 63.

3. Record scores. The students' **fluency score** is the number of words read in 60 seconds, minus the number of errors made during that minute. The **accuracy score** is the number of errors for the entire passage the first time through. Use a different mark for errors on the second time through the passage.

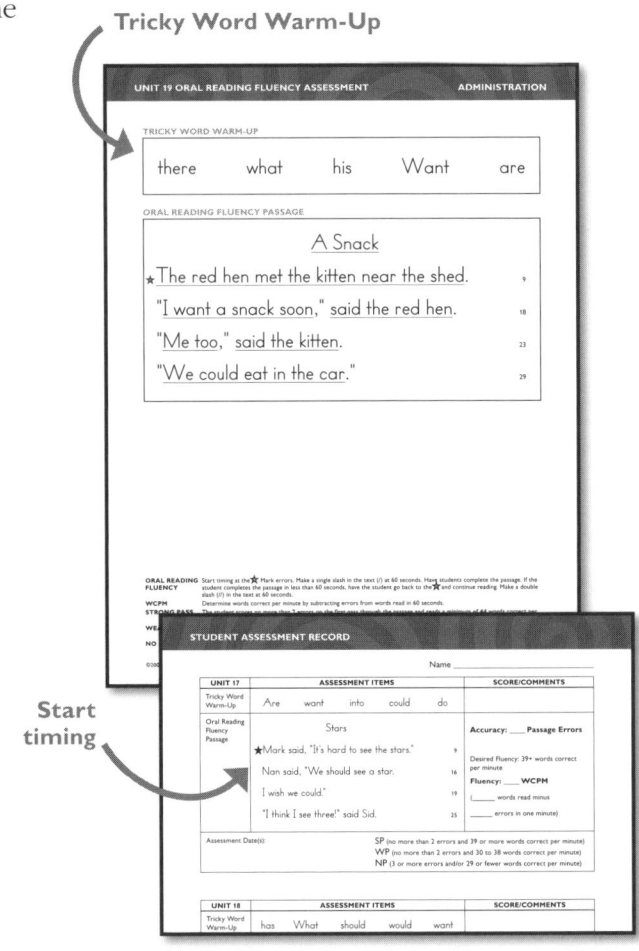

SECTION 3 Ongoing Assessment

Oral Reading Fluency Assessments, Units 16–20

Scoring

DIAGNOSTIC SCORING FOR UNITS 16–20	
If the student . . .	**Record . . .**
Needs Assistance Wait three seconds. Gently tell the student the correct response, draw a line through the item, and write an "A" for "assisted." Score as incorrect response.	Incorrect I hear the ha~~r~~sh wind. (A above)
Mispronounces a Word or Sound Draw a line through the item. Record what the student said. Score as incorrect response.	Incorrect The cat said, "This she~~d~~ is dark and neat." (shack above)
Omits a Word or Word Part Circle the omission. Score as incorrect response.	Incorrect The (red) hen went to ask the cat.
Inserts a Word Write what the student said, using a caret to show where the student inserted the word. Score as incorrect response.	Incorrect Mack said, "I should ask ^my Dad."
Self-Corrects If the student spontaneously self-corrects, write "SC" and score as a correct response.	Correct Where is that nest? (the SC above)
If the student requires more than two attempts, score as an incorrect response.	Incorrect It's in the tr~~e~~e. (a/that/the above)
Repeats Words Underline repeated words.	Correct Mack had to <u>think</u> hard.
Reverses Word Draw a line around the words as shown.	Correct "Sit still," said the man.
SECOND TIME THROUGH	
Any Error	Make a ✓ over each word.	I left the park. (✓ over "left")

63

SECTION 3 Ongoing Assessment

Oral Reading Fluency Assessments, Units 16–20

How to Administer Units 16–20

Following is a sample script for Unit 18.

Tricky Word Warm-Up

Have the student point to and read each word. Say something like:

Touch under the first Tricky Word. Read the word. **(has)**

Read the next word. **(What)**

Repeat with the remaining words.

Oral Reading Fluency Passage

Have the student point to each word and read the title. Say something like:

Read the title for me. **(The Smart Shark)**

What do you think this story is going to be about?

Have the student point to each word and read the passage.

Start timing at the ★.

I'm going to have you read the story about the shark.

I'm going to time you, but I want you to read just like you always do.

Put your finger under the first word. You can start any time you are ready.

Record errors on the Student Assessment Record.

At 60 seconds, make a slash (/) in the text but have the student complete the passage. If the student completes the passage in less than 60 seconds, quickly point to the ★ and say something like:

Wow! Keep reading until I say stop.

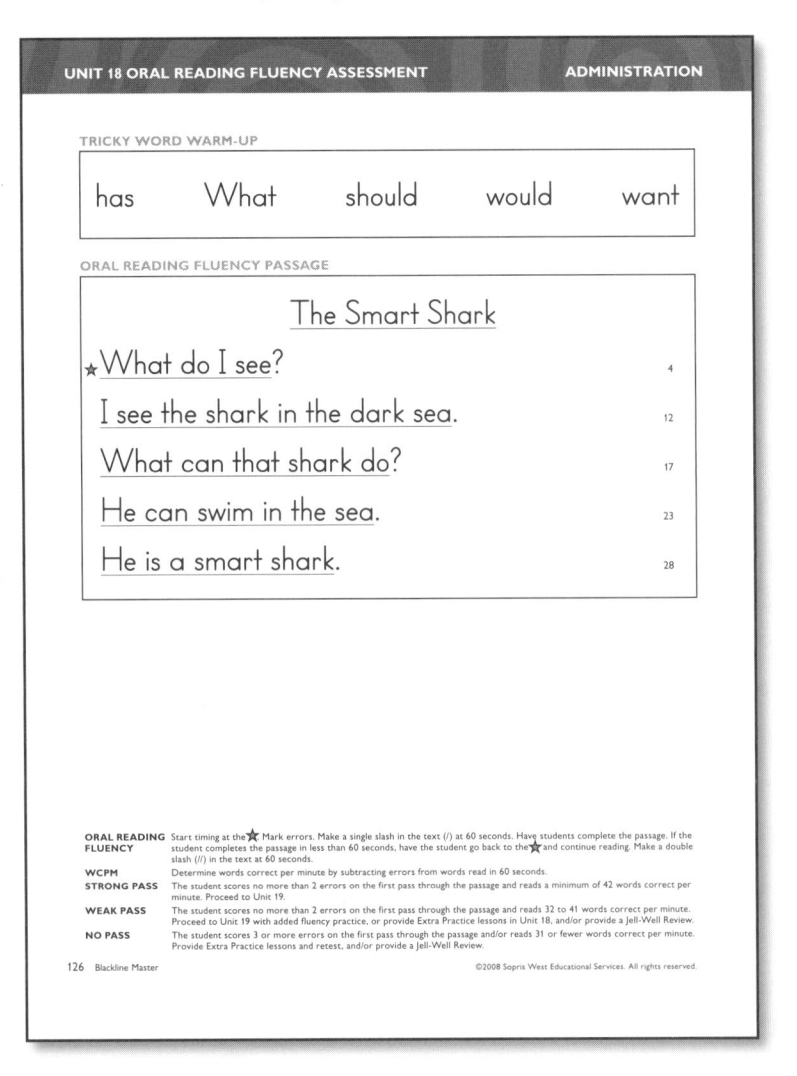

UNIT 18 ORAL READING FLUENCY ASSESSMENT — ADMINISTRATION

TRICKY WORD WARM-UP

| has | What | should | would | want |

ORAL READING FLUENCY PASSAGE

The Smart Shark

★ What do I see? — 4
I see the shark in the dark sea. — 12
What can that shark do? — 17
He can swim in the sea. — 23
He is a smart shark. — 28

ORAL READING FLUENCY — Start timing at the ★. Mark errors. Make a single slash in the text (/) at 60 seconds. Have students complete the passage. If the student completes the passage in less than 60 seconds, have the student go back to the ★ and continue reading. Make a double slash (//) in the text at 60 seconds.

WCPM — Determine words correct per minute by subtracting errors from words read in 60 seconds.

STRONG PASS — The student scores no more than 2 errors on the first pass through the passage and reads a minimum of 42 words correct per minute. Proceed to Unit 19.

WEAK PASS — The student scores no more than 2 errors on the first pass through the passage and reads 32 to 41 words correct per minute. Proceed to Unit 19 with added fluency practice, or provide Extra Practice lessons in Unit 18, and/or provide a Jell-Well Review.

NO PASS — The student scores 3 or more errors on the first pass through the passage and/or reads 31 or fewer words correct per minute. Provide Extra Practice lessons and retest, and/or provide a Jell-Well Review.

126 Blackline Master ©2008 Sopris West Educational Services. All rights reserved.

SECTION 3 — Ongoing Assessment

Oral Reading Fluency Assessments, Units 16–20

Matt's Example

UNIT 18	ASSESSMENT ITEMS	SCORE/COMMENTS
Tricky Word Warm-Up	has What should would want	
Oral Reading Fluency Passage	**The Smart Shark** ★What do I see? 4 I see the shark//in the dark sea. 12 　　　　　　the What can ~~that~~ shark do? 17 He can swim in the sea. 23 　　　　1 He is ~~a~~ smart shark. 28	Accuracy: _2_ Passage Errors Desired Fluency: 42+ words correct per minute Fluency: _34_ WCPM (_36_ words read minus _2_ errors in one minute)
Assessment Date(s): 6/1	SP (no more than 2 errors and 42 or more words correct per minute) (WP) (no more than 2 errors and 32 to 41 words correct per minute) NP (3 or more errors and/or 31 or fewer words correct per minute)	

Alaina's Example

UNIT 18	ASSESSMENT ITEMS	SCORE/COMMENTS
Tricky Word Warm-Up	has What should would want	
Oral Reading Fluency Passage	**The Smart Shark** ★What do I see? 4 I see the shark in the (dark) sea. 12 　　　　　　the What can ~~that~~ shark do? 17 He can swim in the sea. 23 He is//a smart shark. 28	Accuracy: _2_ Passage Errors Desired Fluency: 42+ words correct per minute Fluency: _51_ WCPM (_53_ words read minus _2_ errors in one minute)
Assessment Date(s): 5/22	(SP) (no more than 2 errors and 42 or more words correct per minute) WP (no more than 2 errors and 32 to 41 words correct per minute) NP (3 or more errors and/or 31 or fewer words correct per minute)	

SECTION 3 Ongoing Assessment

Decoding Diagnosis, Unit 20

By Unit 16, the assessments are no longer diagnostic. Instead, the global oral reading fluency score is used to assess progress. If students have difficulty passing the Unit 20 Assessment, the Decoding Diagnosis can be used to more accurately diagnose specific problems.

How to Administer a Decoding Diagnosis

1. Have the student read from the Decoding Diagnosis. Score on a separate copy.
2. For each subtest, have the student point to and read each item.
3. Make a slash through any item the student misses and record what the student said above the missed item.

UNIT 20 DECODING DIAGNOSIS — ADMINISTRATION

SOUNDS

ĕ	Th	r	k	oo	E	ar	wh
i	sh	ee	Wh	a	ĕ	H	ea

VOWEL DISCRIMINATION

| sit / ~~set~~ | sat | set / ~~sit~~ | seat |
| Mark | Mick | Mark / ~~Mack~~ | meek |

BEGINNING QUICK SOUNDS

| dent | hand | test | dark |
| hat / ~~hit~~ | tent | Kim | dish / ~~dash~~ |

BLENDS AND WORD ENDINGS

| Trish | snack | crack / ~~creek~~ | kitten |
| scot / ~~scoot~~ | wham | drank / ~~drink~~ | scat |

TRICKY WORDS

| where | into | as | wouldn't |
| what | to | There | are |

- Have students read from a clean copy of the Decoding Diagnosis. Record incorrect responses on another copy.
- Use information from both the Unit 20 Fluency Assessment and the Unit 20 Decoding Diagnosis to identify specific skill deficits.

©2008 Sopris West Educational Services. All rights reserved.   Blackline Master 129

> **NOTE**
> In this example, the student had difficulty passing Unit 20 Assessment. The teacher administered the Decoding Diagnosis and determined the student is firm on sounds but is not systematically applying them in word reading. See page 86 for prescriptions.

SECTION 4
Making Decisions

This section explains how to adjust instruction to meet the changing needs of your students. Each segment provides information tailored to the developmental progress of students.

Adjusting Instruction	68
Using Assessment Results, Preludes A–C	71
Using Assessment Results, Units 1–5	75
Using Assessment Results, Units 6–15	78
Using Assessment Results, Units 16–20	82
Using a Decoding Diagnosis	86
Group Record Keeping	88

Every *Read Well* teacher is a diagnostician.

SECTION 4 — Making Decisions

Adjusting Instruction

Many factors may affect students' progress. Assessment results help you adjust instruction and practice to meet the changing needs of your children. *Read Well* assessment results assist you in determining when to accelerate groups and/or individuals and when to develop interventions for groups and/or individuals.

Analyzing Scores

Copy assessment scores from students' Assessment Records to the Group Assessment Record. (As subtests vary across units, several different forms are provided. See pages 142–149.)

The Group Assessment Record allows you to:

- Analyze the strengths and weaknesses of a group of students
- Compare the progress of individual students with the group
- Quickly share assessment results with colleagues
- Make regrouping decisions

Units	No Pass	Pass
Preludes A–C	Accuracy and Comprehension Only Assessed	
1–5	Accuracy Only Assessed	

Unit	No Pass	Weak Pass	Strong Pass
6	Fails to meet goals on 2 or more subtests	Meets 4/5 subtests and/or fails fluency	Meets all subtests and 24–27 WCPM*
7	↓	Meets 4/5 subtests and/or fails fluency	Meets all subtests and 24–27 WCPM*
8		Meets 4/5 subtests and/or fails fluency	Meets all subtests and 21–24 WCPM
9		Meets 3/4 subtests and/or fails fluency	Meets all subtests and 22–24 WCPM
10		Meets 3/4 subtests and/or fails fluency	Meets all subtests and 22–24 WCPM
11		Meets 3/4 subtests and/or fails fluency	Meets all subtests and 24–26 WCPM
12		Meets 3/4 subtests and/or fails fluency	Meets all subtests and 26–28 WCPM
13		Meets 3/4 subtests and/or fails fluency	Meets all subtests and 28–30 WCPM
14		Meets 3/4 subtests and/or fails fluency	Meets all subtests and 30–32 WCPM
15		Meets 3/4 subtests and/or fails fluency	Meets all subtests and 34–36 WCPM

Unit	No Pass WCPM	Weak Pass WCPM	Strong Pass WCPM
16	27 or fewer	28–35	36+
17	29 or fewer	30–38	39+
18	31 or fewer	32–41	42+
19	33 or fewer	34–43	44+
20	35 or fewer	36–45	46+

*The assessments for Units 6 and 7 include a picture word, which makes the assessment easier and the word count per minute higher.

STRONG PASS • ACCELERATION

Consecutive Strong Passes or high fluency scores may indicate that a student can move to a higher-performing group. Consecutive Strong Passes by a group may indicate that the pace of instruction should be accelerated.

WEAK PASS • PREVENTION

A Weak Pass provides an important red flag. This score indicates a child in potential trouble.

As soon as you see a Weak Pass, a quick and low-keyed prescription can prevent future failure. If a child receives consecutive Weak Passes, then No Passes are a certainty in the future.

Prescriptions may be as simple as:

- Reading a Solo Story to a peer before lunch and before going home
- Sitting in with a lower-performing group for a second dose of reading
- Reading Solo Stories at home
- Reading Solo Stories each day into a tape recorder.

SECTION 4: Making Decisions
Adjusting Instruction

At the end of each unit, review your Group Assessment Record. If you regroup between classrooms (walk-to-read), meet on a regular basis to share results, problem solve, and regroup students, as appropriate.

GENERAL PRESCRIPTIONS

Who	Score	Then . . .
An entire small group	Strong Pass	Continue forward. Consider a faster pace of instruction.
Part of a small group Individuals		Consider regrouping for acceleration.
An entire small group	Pass	Continue forward at the same pace of instruction.
Part of a small group Individuals		Consider regrouping. (See prescriptions for students with Weak and No Passes.)
An entire small group	Weak Pass	Practice a difficult skill throughout the day with the whole class. Emphasize instruction and practice on any difficult skills while: • Providing Extra Practice lessons for the unit • Reteaching lessons or the unit
Part of a small group Individuals		Consider regrouping. Provide a second dose of instruction for these students. Emphasize instruction and practice on any difficult skills while: • Providing Extra Practice lessons for the unit • Reteaching lessons or the unit • Previewing the next unit
An entire small group Part of a small group Individuals	No Pass	Consider regrouping. Provide a second dose of instruction for these students. Emphasize instruction and practice on any difficult skills while: • Providing Extra Practice lessons for the unit • Reteaching lessons or the unit • Previewing the next unit • Providing a Jell-Well Review of previous units (see Section 5)

STRONG PASS/PASS

Most students will receive Strong Passes and Passes when placed appropriately, grouped appropriately, given sufficient instructional time, and taught well.

SECTION 4 — Making Decisions
Adjusting Instruction

Double Dosing

Read Well's flexible construction makes it possible to help children become independent readers at an optimum rate. Schools often give some children a double dose of *Read Well* instruction to maximize progress.

A double dose of *Read Well* instruction may be provided:

FOR	BY	WHEN	WITH
• A group • Part of a group • An individual student	• Another teacher (classroom or specialist) • Paraprofessional • Parent volunteer • Older student • Peer	• Before school • After school • During school	• Additional *Read Well* lessons within a day • Extra practice within a unit • Preteaching lessons • Reteaching lessons • Remediation of a skill • Jell-Well Review (recycling)

Note: In some cases, schools intervene aggressively with a triple dose of *Read Well* instruction and practice for the highest-risk students.

SECTION 4 — Making Decisions

Using Assessment Results, Preludes A-C

Preludes A–C provide direct instruction in basic readiness skills—one-to-one correspondence between a symbol and a word, tracking, recognition of common school objects, learning what a sound is, phonemic awareness, and identifying who a story is about.

Pass/No Pass

At the bottom of each assessment, you will find criteria for a Pass or No Pass and instructions for what to do next. For example, at the bottom of the Prelude C Assessment, the instructions indicate that children who pass should proceed to Unit 1, and children who do not pass should begin Extra Practice lessons.

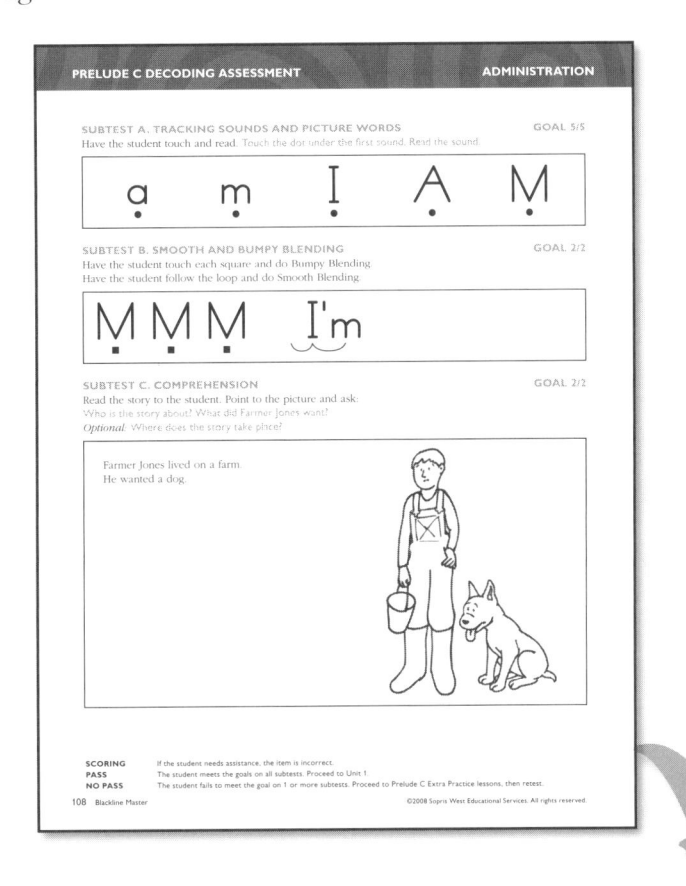

SAMPLE: PRELUDE C

Pass	The student meets the goals on all subtests. Proceed to Unit 1.
No Pass	The student fails to meet the goals for 1 or more subtests. Proceed to Prelude C Extra Practice lessons, then retest.

SECTION 4 **Making Decisions**
Using Assessment Results, Preludes A–C

Intervention Flow Chart

Students who require intervention to pass the Preludes may need additional instruction as they proceed through *Read Well K*. The flow chart demonstrates how to provide ongoing intervention using assessment results and *Read Well K* Extra Practice.

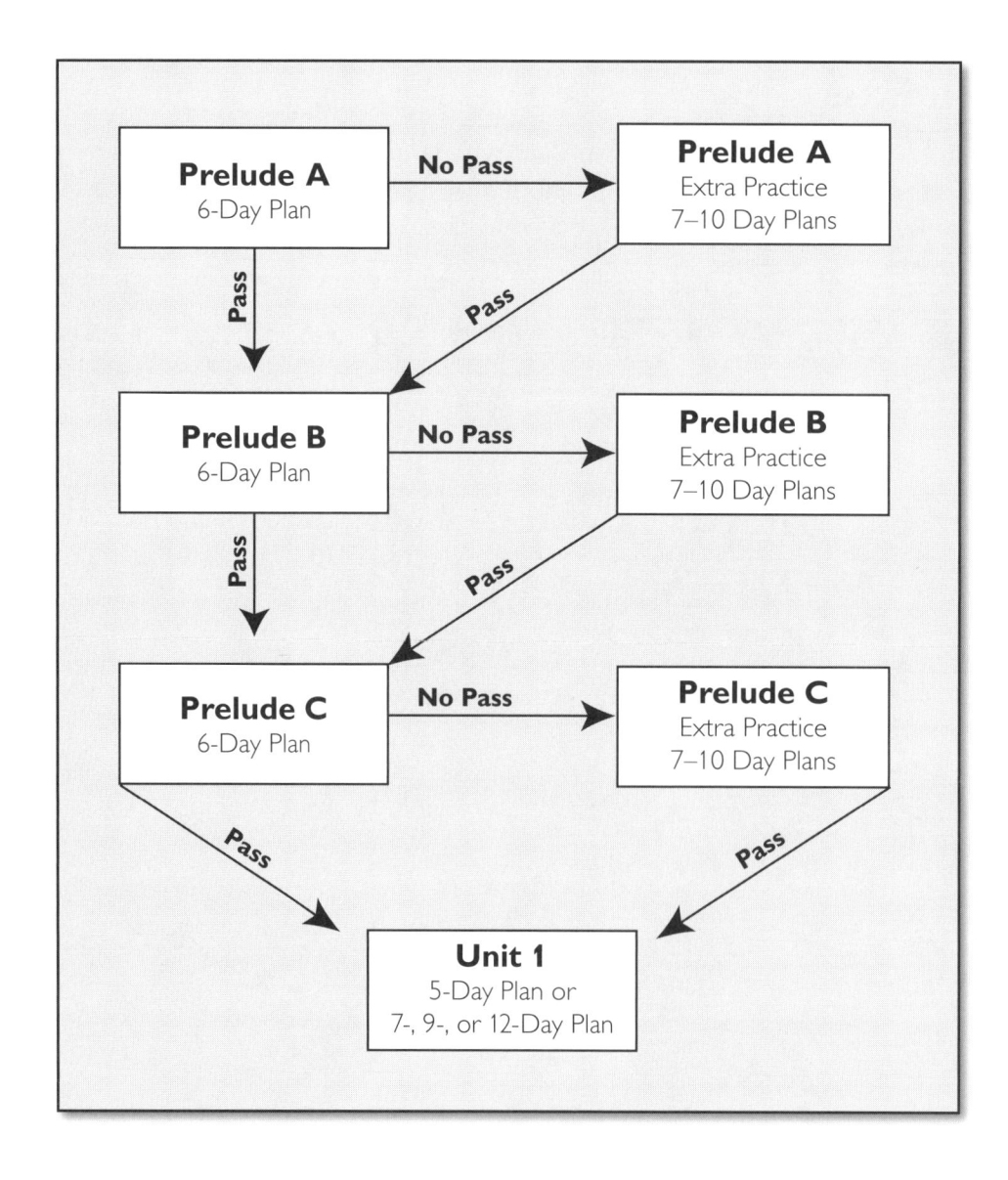

```
Prelude A            No Pass      Prelude A
6-Day Plan          ─────────▶    Extra Practice
     │                            7–10 Day Plans
     │ Pass                            │
     ▼            Pass                 │
Prelude B            No Pass      Prelude B
6-Day Plan          ─────────▶    Extra Practice
     │                            7–10 Day Plans
     │ Pass                            │
     ▼            Pass                 │
Prelude C            No Pass      Prelude C
6-Day Plan          ─────────▶    Extra Practice
     │                            7–10 Day Plans
     │ Pass                            │
     │                                 │ Pass
     ▼                                 ▼
              Unit 1
          5-Day Plan or
        7-, 9-, or 12-Day Plan
```

SECTION 4 — Making Decisions
Using Assessment Results, Preludes A–C

Diagnostic–Prescriptive Teaching

When students have difficulty, diagnose or pinpoint error patterns. Provide an increased instructional focus on the weak skills while maintaining a balanced daily lesson. Examples follow.

SPECIFIC PRESCRIPTIONS FOR PRELUDES A–C

If students have difficulty with...	Then try these prescriptions...
Finger Tracking	• Use Finger Tracking Games such as *Simon Says*. • Motivate young children to track text with little gimmicks, such as *witch fingers* placed on those who track text. • Pay more attention to students who are tracking than those who are not—"Martha gets a turn all by herself because she is doing Finger Tracking." • Seat children so that you can guide the hands of those most in need of assistance.
Smooth Blending	Have the whole class practice phonemic awareness skills informally throughout the day using: • Stretch and Shrink with names • Smooth and Bumpy Blending with "I" • Stretch and Shrink games: How long can you stretch out "I"? Ensure that the adults teaching this skill can do Stretch and Shrink without stopping between sounds. Practice as needed. Work with individuals on Stretch and Shrink and Sound Counting. Demonstrate, guide, and have the student practice independent of your voice.

(continued)

INSTRUCTION THAT WORKS FOR ALL CHILDREN

Important Instructional Guideline

Teach to the lowest-performing student in each group but adjust groups and individual interventions frequently, so that all children are in developmentally appropriate groups.

SECTION 4: Making Decisions

Using Assessment Results, Preludes A–C

SPECIFIC PRESCRIPTIONS FOR PRELUDES A–C (continued)

If students have difficulty with...	Then try these prescriptions...

Sound and Word Recognition	• Write the word or sound on a card.
	• Tape the card on the child's desk with a sticky note covering it.
	
	Ham it up! Have the classroom teacher, paraprofessional, and volunteers working in the room ask the student to peek under the sticky note throughout the day and tell what the secret sound or word is.
	
	Say something like:
	   Let's look under your sticky note.
	   What's your secret sound?
	
	Later in the day, say:
	   Oh dear! I've forgotten what your secret sound is. Let's look at it.
	   What's your secret sound?

Comprehension	Have a volunteer work with one or two students each day if they have difficulty identifying who the story is about in Subtest D. Have the volunteer read a short picture book to the student or students, frequently asking "Who is the story about?" Once students can identify who a story is about with different books, have the volunteer add the following prompt: "What is [Farmer Jones] doing?" and "What does [Farmer Jones] want?" Eventually, questions about the sequence of events or action can be added.

DISTRIBUTE PRACTICE

Frequent practice within a day and across days can help students develop the depth of knowledge required for long-term retention.

SECTION 4 — Making Decisions

Using Assessment Results, Units 1–5

Units 1–5 create a foundation of learning for later units. Mastery in the early units is critical for success in the remaining units.

Pass/No Pass

At the bottom of each assessment for Units 1–5, you will find the criteria for a Pass or No Pass. The criteria remain high through the early units.

SAMPLE: UNIT 3	
Pass	The student meets the goals on all subtests. Proceed to Unit 4.
No Pass	The student fails to meet the goals on 1 or more subtests. Provide Extra Practice lessons and retest and/or administer assessments from earlier units to determine where to begin a Jell-Well Review.

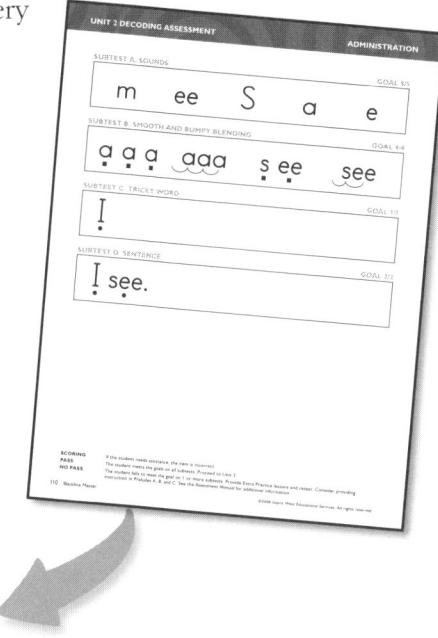

This flow chart demonstrates how to plan instruction based on student performance.

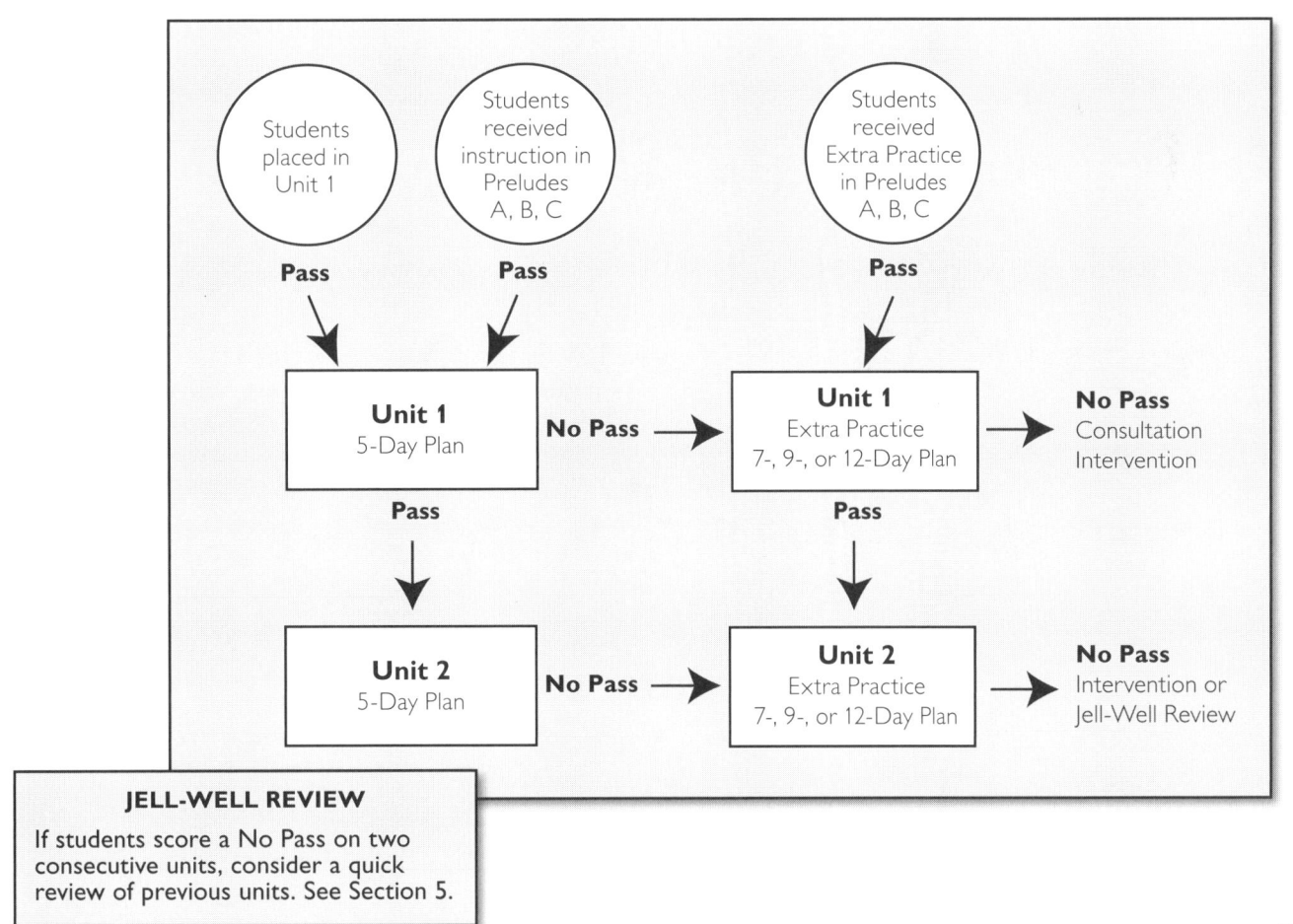

- Students placed in Unit 1 — **Pass** →
- Students received instruction in Preludes A, B, C — **Pass** →

Unit 1 5-Day Plan — **No Pass** → **Unit 1** Extra Practice 7-, 9-, or 12-Day Plan — **No Pass** → Consultation Intervention

- Students received Extra Practice in Preludes A, B, C — **Pass** ↓

Pass ↓

Unit 2 5-Day Plan — **No Pass** → **Unit 2** Extra Practice 7-, 9-, or 12-Day Plan — **No Pass** → Intervention or Jell-Well Review

JELL-WELL REVIEW

If students score a No Pass on two consecutive units, consider a quick review of previous units. See Section 5.

SECTION 4 — Making Decisions
Using Assessment Results, Units 1–5

Diagnostic–Prescriptive Teaching

If students have difficulty with a specific skill, focus instruction on weak skills while maintaining practice on all skills. Examples follow.

SPECIFIC PRESCRIPTIONS FOR UNITS 1–5	
If students have difficulty with . . .	**Then try these prescriptions . . .**
Smooth Blending	Seek peer consultation if all students do not pass Subtest B, Smooth and Bumpy Blending, in Unit 2. You may find that you have been stopping between sounds as you model. If so, work with a colleague and reteach.
Smooth Blending With a Beginning Quick Sound	• Provide Extra Practice Lesson 1 with additional practice blending /d/. • Provide repeated practice with the Smooth and Bumpy Blending Card 11. • Give each student in the group a special practice card. **PRACTICE CARD** I can blend "Dad" smoothly. Listen to me really *ssstrrreeetch* out the word, without pausing between the sounds. When I do this, please initial one of the boxes. Dad ☐ ☐ ☐ ☐ ☐ If students rapidly master the difficult skill, reassess as soon as possible. A day or two of intense practice may be sufficient to master a difficult skill.

SECTION 4 — Making Decisions
Using Assessment Results, Units 1–5

SPECIFIC PRESCRIPTIONS FOR UNITS 1–5 (continued)

If students have difficulty with . . .	Then try these prescriptions . . .
Smooth Blending Beginning Quick Sound /d/	Have the whole class practice blending "dad" throughout the day and across days. Provide practice with: • Stretch and Shrink with /dăăăd/ • dad • Smooth and Bumpy Blending with "dad" • Dictation on white boards with: dad, sad, mad
Tricky Word Recognition	• Write the word or sound on the child's hand with a washable marker. • Have the student read his or her special word to others throughout the day and use the word in a sentence. Say something like: Show me your special word. What's your word? (said) What did Mrs. Jones say? (It's time for recess.) Say "Mrs. Jones said, 'It's time for recess.'" (Mrs. Jones said, "It's time for recess.")

TAILORING PRACTICE INSTRUCTIONAL GUIDELINE

Most children who have difficulty in the early units will have difficulty with Smooth Blending. In later units, difficulty is often with fluency. Tailor interventions to the specific skill needs of the student.

SECTION 4 Making Decisions
Using Assessment Results, Units 6–15

Units 6–15 strengthen and build on the skills learned in Units 1–5. In Unit 6, a desired fluency goal is added to the subtest on sentence reading.

Note: The goal of instruction in Units 6–15 is not speed. The goal is accuracy and mastery of blending. However, the added fluency measure objectively assesses students' developing skills. Students who are not able to meet the desired fluency goals need more intensive practice.

Strong Pass, Weak Pass, No Pass

At the bottom of each assessment for Units 6–15, you will find the criteria for a Strong Pass, a Weak Pass, and a No Pass.

	SAMPLE: UNIT 6
Strong Pass	The student meets the goals on all subtests and has attained the desired fluency. Proceed to Unit 7.
Weak Pass	The student meets the goals on 4 out of 5 subtests and/or fails to attain the desired fluency. Proceed to Unit 7 with added practice on difficult skills, or provide Extra Practice lessons in Unit 6, and/or provide a Jell-Well Review.
No Pass	The student fails to meet the goals on 2 or more subtests. Provide Extra Practice lessons and retest, and/or provide a Jell-Well Review.

In Preludes A–C and Units 1–5, the sample Pass/No Pass system provides sufficient information to ensure that a strong foundation is established. The new Strong Pass/Weak Pass/No Pass system in these later units provides additional instructional options.

- Consistent Strong Passes signal the possibility of moving faster.
- A Weak Pass indicates the need for additional work to achieve mastery.

  Weak Passes for two consecutive units are an indication that, without intervention, future difficulties are likely. With repeated Weak Passes, the student's burden of learning will eventually become overwhelming. A Weak Pass is a red flag.

- A No Pass indicates the need for immediate intervention.

Intervention

Early intervention is strongly recommended as it serves as a basis for later learning. Time spent on building mastery in the early units will result in faster mastery in later units and will prevent students from becoming overwhelmed.

SECTION 4 — Making Decisions
Using Assessment Results, Units 6–15

Intervention Flow Chart

This flow chart demonstrates how to plan instruction based on student performance.

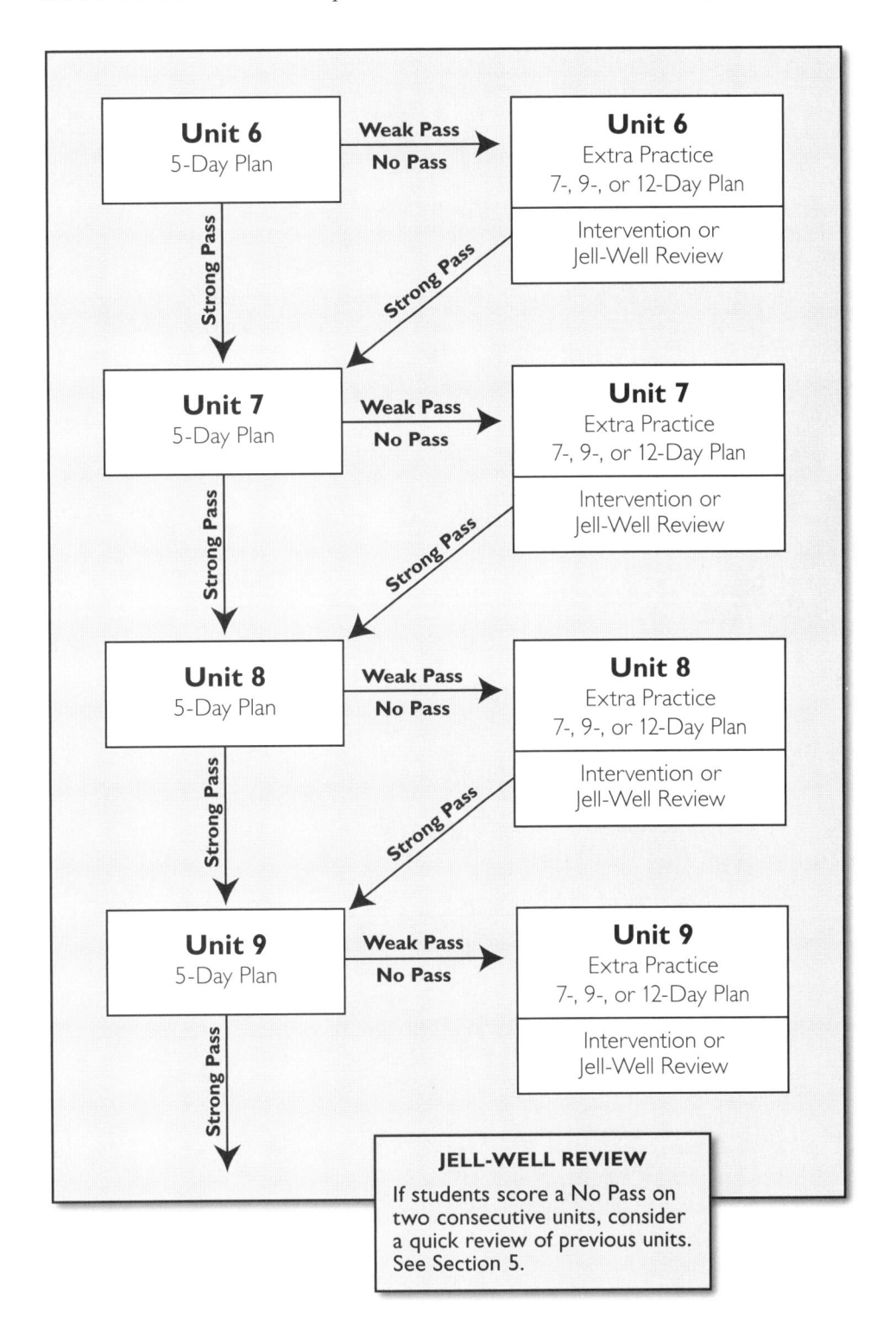

```
┌─────────────┐   Weak Pass    ┌──────────────────────┐
│  Unit 6     │ ─────────────► │  Unit 6              │
│  5-Day Plan │   No Pass      │  Extra Practice      │
└─────────────┘                │  7-, 9-, or 12-Day   │
      │                        │  Plan                │
      │ Strong Pass            ├──────────────────────┤
      │                        │  Intervention or     │
      │         ◄── Strong ──  │  Jell-Well Review    │
      ▼           Pass         └──────────────────────┘
┌─────────────┐   Weak Pass    ┌──────────────────────┐
│  Unit 7     │ ─────────────► │  Unit 7              │
│  5-Day Plan │   No Pass      │  Extra Practice      │
└─────────────┘                │  7-, 9-, or 12-Day   │
      │                        │  Plan                │
      │ Strong Pass            ├──────────────────────┤
      │                        │  Intervention or     │
      │         ◄── Strong ──  │  Jell-Well Review    │
      ▼           Pass         └──────────────────────┘
┌─────────────┐   Weak Pass    ┌──────────────────────┐
│  Unit 8     │ ─────────────► │  Unit 8              │
│  5-Day Plan │   No Pass      │  Extra Practice      │
└─────────────┘                │  7-, 9-, or 12-Day   │
      │                        │  Plan                │
      │ Strong Pass            ├──────────────────────┤
      │                        │  Intervention or     │
      │         ◄── Strong ──  │  Jell-Well Review    │
      ▼           Pass         └──────────────────────┘
┌─────────────┐   Weak Pass    ┌──────────────────────┐
│  Unit 9     │ ─────────────► │  Unit 9              │
│  5-Day Plan │   No Pass      │  Extra Practice      │
└─────────────┘                │  7-, 9-, or 12-Day   │
      │                        │  Plan                │
      │ Strong Pass            ├──────────────────────┤
      ▼                        │  Intervention or     │
                               │  Jell-Well Review    │
                               └──────────────────────┘
```

JELL-WELL REVIEW

If students score a No Pass on two consecutive units, consider a quick review of previous units. See Section 5.

SECTION 4 Making Decisions
Using Assessment Results, Units 6–15

Diagnostic–Prescriptive Teaching

Continue to diagnose or pinpoint error patterns. Following are examples of prescriptions for implementation with groups or individuals:

SPECIFIC PRESCRIPTIONS FOR UNITS 6–15

If students have difficulty with . . .	Then try these prescriptions . . .
A Sound (/ĭĭĭ/)	a. During Sound Card practice, add four more cards with the small letter i. Each time i comes up, have students stop and think before responding. Provide descriptive feedback, referring to the key word for /ĭĭĭ/. Say something like: Let's see if you can get the hard sound /ĭĭĭ/ four times. You got the hard sound—/ĭĭĭ/ as in insect—once. You got the hard sound—/ĭĭĭ/ as in insect—twice. You got the hard sound—/ĭĭĭ/ as in insect—three times. You got the hard sound—/ĭĭĭ/ as in insect—four times! b. During Decoding Practice, have students see who can sustain the sound /ĭĭĭ/ the longest. c. During Accuracy and Fluency practice, have students read the sound twice in rhythm and then read the word. /ĭ/, /ĭ/, in /ĭ/, /ĭ/, tin /ĭ/, /ĭ/, win d. If students have difficulty with /ĭ/, place a card on each child's desk with the letter i and a picture of insects. Make six spaces on the card for someone to initial. • Assign each student with a study buddy who sits nearby. • Teach the study buddy to say: 　Tell me your special sound and word.　(/ĭ/ as in insect) • Teach the study buddy to assist if needed, compliment the child, and initial the card. • When the card is completed, provide each child with something to acknowledge his or her efforts.
Smooth Blending	• Using the same words, precede Smooth Blending with Stretch and Shrink. • Provide additional practice with Smooth and Bumpy Blending. (Make new cards for any difficult words.) • Have students identify whether you are doing Smooth or Bumpy Blending. • Work briefly with individuals, demonstrating, guiding practice, and providing individual turns.

SECTION 4: Making Decisions

Using Assessment Results, Units 6–15

SPECIFIC PRESCRIPTIONS FOR UNITS 6–15 (continued)

If students have difficulty with . . . | **Then try these prescriptions . . .**

Tricky Words (would, could, should)

Practice orally spelling one or two difficult Tricky Words or a Tricky Word pattern.

- Day 1: Write "would," "could," and "should" on the board. Have the class orally spell the words in the morning, before lunch, after lunch, and before going home.

- Day 2: Erase the w, c, and sh from each word, replacing the letters with dashes (i.e., -ould). Have the class orally spell the words in the morning, before lunch, after lunch, and before going home.

- Day 3: Write each word on a card. Have students who know the words dictate the words from the cards. Have the class orally spell the words. Say something like:

    [Charlie], please dictate the first word. (would)
    I *would* like to eat soon. [Charlie], say the word. (would)
    Everyone, spell *would*. (w-o-u-l-d)

    [Yun], please dictate the next word. (could)
    I *could* read the book. [Yun], say the word. (could)
    Everyone, spell *could*. (c-o-u-l-d)

    [Ruth], please dictate the next word. (should)
    I *should* do my best.
    [Ruth], say the word. (should)
    Everyone, spell *should*. (s-h-o-u-l-d)

- Day 4: Erase "-ould" from the board. Have students who have had difficulty assist you with dictation. Have the class orally spell the words.

- Day 5: Have students who have had difficulty assist you with dictation. Have the class write the words on paper or on white boards.

Fluency

a. Begin each day's lesson with five minutes of sustained independent practice.
   - Provide each student with a notebook or booklet of *Read Well* Homework Stories.
   - Have each student point to the words and whisper read for five minutes. Students should begin with Unit 2 and read stories consecutively.
   - Each child's goal is to read a little more each day. Each child can mark where he or she is at the end of five minutes with a sticky note.

b. Begin each day's story reading with a review of the previous day's story.

c. Select paragraphs from review stories for Short Passage Practice. Demonstrate expressive reading. Guide reading. Have individuals read the passage.

d. Review homework procedures. A grade-level routine and full implementation of recommended procedures can result in nearly 100% success with homework completion.

SECTION 4 Making Decisions

Using Assessment Results, Units 16-20

Units 16–20 strengthen and build on the skills learned in Units 1–15. In Unit 16, assessments shift from diagnostic Decoding Assessments to Oral Reading Fluency Assessments.

Strong Pass, Weak Pass, No Pass

At the bottom of each assessment, you will find the criteria for a Strong Pass, Weak Pass, and a No Pass.

	SAMPLE: UNIT 16
Strong Pass	The student scores no more than 2 errors on the first pass through the passage and reads a minimum of 36 words correct per minute. Proceed to Unit 17.
Weak Pass	The student scores no more than 2 errors on the first pass through the passage and reads 28 to 35 words correct per minute. Proceed to Unit 17 with added fluency practice, or provide Extra Practice lessons in Unit 16, and/or provide a Jell-Well Review.
No Pass	The student scores 3 or more errors on the first pass through the passage and/or reads 27 or fewer words correct per minute. Provide Extra Practice lessons and retest, and/or provide a Jell-Well Review.

By this level, students who score a Strong Pass are gaining fluency rapidly with little effort.

- Consistent Strong Passes signal the possibility of moving faster and skipping some consonant units.
- A Weak Pass indicates the need for additional work to achieve mastery.

  Weak Passes on two consecutive units are an indication that future difficulties are likely without intervention. With repeated Weak Passes, the student's burden of learning will eventually become overwhelming.

- A No Pass indicates the need for immediate intervention.

Intervention

Continue to provide intervention, as needed. In Units 16–20, students who are accurate sometimes fail to gain fluency without added assistance.

SECTION 4 — Making Decisions

Using Assessment Results, Units 16–20

Research Snapshot

ORAL READING FLUENCY

Research has shown that oral reading fluency can be a stronger measure of comprehension than traditionally used classroom assessments for reading comprehension. Fuchs, Fuchs, and Maxwell (1988) found a significantly higher correlation between oral reading fluency and the Comprehension Subtest of the Stanford Reading Achievement Test than for traditional direct measures of comprehension (e.g., question answering, passage recall, and cloze).

Samuels and Flor (1997) explain the power of oral reading fluency in reading comprehension. "It is the development of automatic processing in reading that allows our mind to naturally make connections to other prior experiences or knowledge while reading, that allows questions and hypotheses to emerge, and that gives us the ability to pause as we read and to reflect on deeper meanings . . . " (p. 119).

This flow chart demonstrates how to plan instruction based on student performance.

Unit 16 5-Day Plan → Weak Pass / No Pass → **Unit 16** Extra Practice 7-, 9-, or 12-Day Plan / Intervention or Jell-Well Review
↓ Strong Pass (from either path)

Unit 17 5-Day Plan → Weak Pass / No Pass → **Unit 17** Extra Practice 7-, 9-, or 12-Day Plan / Intervention or Jell-Well Review
↓ Strong Pass

Unit 18 5-Day Plan → Weak Pass / No Pass → **Unit 18** Extra Practice 7-, 9-, or 12-Day Plan / Intervention or Jell-Well Review
↓ Strong Pass

Unit 19 5-Day Plan → Weak Pass / No Pass → **Unit 19** Extra Practice 7-, 9-, or 12-Day Plan / Intervention or Jell-Well Review
↓ Strong Pass

Unit 20 5-Day Plan → Weak Pass / No Pass → **Unit 20** Extra Practice 7-, 9-, or 12-Day Plan / Intervention or Jell-Well Review

---

JELL-WELL REVIEW

If students score a No Pass on two consecutive units, consider a quick review of previous units. See Section 5.

SECTION 4 Making Decisions
Using Assessment Results, Units 16–20

Diagnostic–Prescriptive Teaching

SPECIFIC PRESCRIPTIONS FOR UNITS 16–20	
If students have difficulty with . . .	**Then try these prescriptions . . .**
Reading Accurately	Focus on reducing careless errors, repetitions, and self-corrections during oral reading. Follow these steps: a. Provide an Extra Practice lesson. b. After students read the story, have the children listen to you read. Tell students that they can raise their hands (or mark their stories with a simple slash) when they hear you make an error. Model each of the following types of errors: • Reading a word incorrectly • Leaving out a word Explain that it is important to read words accurately and only once. Tell students they should also count the following as errors: • Making corrections • Repeating a word Read the passage slowly. Make errors and ham it up. The children will love it. c. Have students read the passage with individual turns on sentences. Quietly count errors. d. After the reading is complete, review the errors without identifying individuals. Have students practice reading the sentences accurately. Have students reread the passage. The goal is to improve students' accuracy. e. Acknowledge accomplishments.

SECTION 4 — Making Decisions

Using Assessment Results, Units 16–20

SPECIFIC PRESCRIPTIONS FOR UNITS 16–20 (continued)

If students have difficulty with . . .   **Then try these prescriptions . . .**

Tricky Words

Spelling and Discrimination Practice

Follow these steps for correcting problems with "where" and "were."

- Days 1, 2: Write "wHere" on the board. Have the class orally spell "where" by letter names, saying the H loudly. Practice each time the class lines up.

- Day 3: Have five students write a "Where?" question on the board for the class to read and answer.

- Day 4: Have each student write "where" on the board or during white board practice.

- Day 5: Make a color shade. Find a simple blackline drawing. Draw lines in the picture, creating shapes that can be colored. Write "where" in all the spaces.

  Draw shapes in the space outside the picture. Write "were" in each of these shapes.

  Make a copy for each child. Have students color all the spaces with "where."

- Days 6, 7: Practice spelling "where" *and* "were" orally.

  Repeat Days 3–5 using "where" and "were."

Fluency

Extending Units With Repeated Readings

a. Extend lessons (e.g., if students are working on 5-Day Plans, implement 7-Day Plans). Spend more time on repeated readings of Solo Stories.
   - After practicing the Solo Story with choral reading and individual turns on sentences, give each student a turn to read a page.
   - Set an accuracy goal of 0–2 errors.
   - To motivate practice, give each student a transparency and a marker. Have students follow along and mark errors as individuals take turns. Have the strongest readers read first. Model giving compliments. Have one or two students give a compliment to each child.

b. Set up repeated reading sessions with a tutor.
   - Set an accuracy goal of 0–2 errors.
   - Have the student read an *easy* Solo Story for accuracy.
   - When the student is able to read within the accuracy goal, time the passage reading.
   - Congratulate the child each time his or her fluency improves.

SECTION 4 — Making Decisions

Using a Decoding Diagnosis

At Unit 16, the Oral Reading Fluency measure takes the place of the Decoding Assessment. If a student has difficulty meeting the Oral Reading Fluency goal, additional diagnostic information may be of use in determining how to remediate skill deficiencies. A Decoding Diagnosis is included after the Unit 20 Assessment.

Note: If a student is unable to meet the Oral Reading Fluency goal, he or she may have been misplaced initially, or instruction may have proceeded too fast in the earlier units. If the student makes errors related to one or two skills, you may be able to remediate these skills with intensive work. However, if the student is weak on three or more skills, he or she will need either a careful Jell-Well Review or placement in a lower group.

Guidelines for Remediating Specific Skills

Sounds

- If the student misses only one sound, continue to the next unit but provide additional practice on that sound.
- If the student makes more than one error, consider placing the student in a lower group, providing a Jell-Well Review, or systematically reintroducing one new difficult sound at a time.

Vowel Discrimination

- Have the student practice words that require vowel discrimination. Build lists of words composed of known sounds, in which only the vowel changes (e.g., m<u>e</u>t, m<u>a</u>t, m<u>ea</u>t). See the subtest examples.
- Provide additional practice on all the vowel sounds taught to date. Reteach all vowel units, while repeatedly reviewing all known sounds.

Beginning Quick Sounds

- Have the student practice pairs of rhyming words in which one word begins with a quick sound (e.g., went–<u>d</u>ent, sand–<u>h</u>and).
- Have the student practice lists of words that begin with one quick sound (e.g., had–hid–hard).
- Reteach all units that introduce a quick sound and review all known sounds.

Blends and Word Endings

- Have the student read lists of words that increase in length and that include difficult blends and/or word endings (e.g., ack–nack–snack, kit–kitten).
- Dictate words that build up (e.g., in, ink, rink, drink).

Tricky Words

- Identify the difficult words and increase practice on one difficult word at a time.
- Have the student write any difficult word and use it in a sentence.

SECTION 4 — Making Decisions
Using a Decoding Diagnosis

UNIT 20 DECODING DIAGNOSIS — ADMINISTRATION

SOUNDS

ĕ	Th	r	k	oo	E	ar	wh
i	sh	ee	Wh	a	ĕ	H	ea

VOWEL DISCRIMINATION

set	sat	sit	seat
Mark	Mick	Mack	meek

BEGINNING QUICK SOUNDS

dent	hand	test	dark
hit	tent	Kim	dash

BLENDS AND WORD ENDINGS

Trish	snack	creek	kitten
scoot	wham	drink	scat

TRICKY WORDS

where	into	as	wouldn't
what	to	There	are

- Have students read from a clean copy of the Decoding Diagnosis. Record incorrect responses on another copy.
- Use information from both the Unit 20 Fluency Assessment and the Unit 20 Decoding Diagnosis to identify specific skill deficits.

©2008 Sopris West Educational Services. All rights reserved.

Blackline Master 129

SECTION 4 Making Decisions

Group Record Keeping

Description

Read Well K includes a Student Assessment Record, which you can copy for each child, and optional Group Assessment Records. The Student Assessment Record provides a place for you to score responses and also provides a continuous record of an individual student's progress. (See pages 130–141.) By contrast, the Group Assessment Records will include scores for all children in a group. The Group Assessment Records allow you to see the strengths and weaknesses of a group of students, providing important instructional information. Pages 139–147 include blackline masters of Group Assessment Records. As the subtests vary across units, several different forms are provided. Additional forms can be copied, and additional spaces are provided in case you need to extend practice and reassess.

- Group Assessment Record • Prelude A
- Group Assessment Record • Preludes B and C
- Group Assessment Record • Unit 1
- Group Assessment Record • Units 2–4
- Group Assessment Record • Unit 5
- Group Assessment Record • Units 6–8
- Group Assessment Record • Units 9–15
- Group Assessment Record • Units 16–20

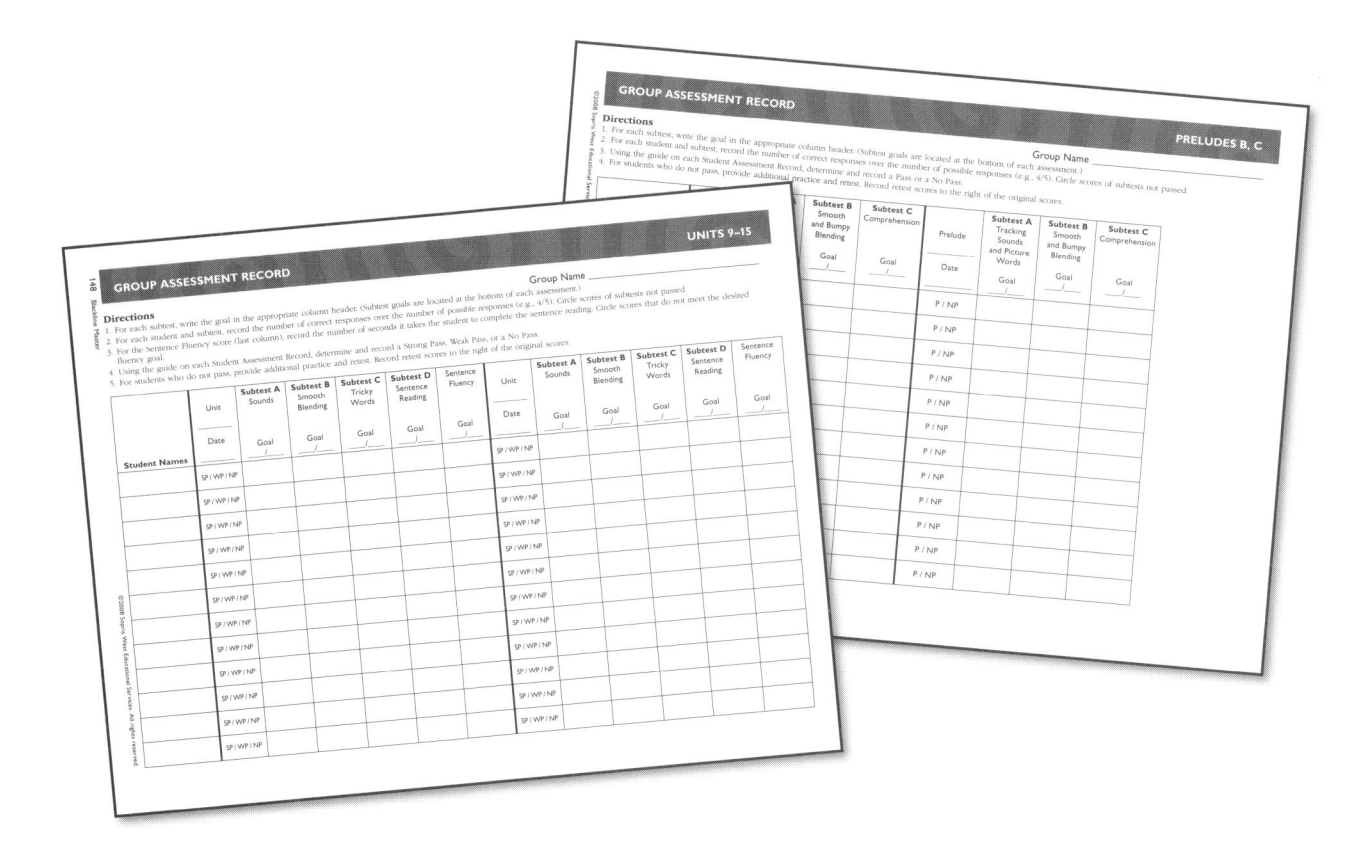

SECTION 4 — Making Decisions

Group Record Keeping

Using the Group Record Form to Inform Practice

Sydney's Scenario

At the beginning of the year, Sydney knew 16 letter names, no sounds, and no words. Sydney placed in Mrs. Jones' Group 2. Sydney's group completed Preludes A, B, and C, with all members passing the three Preludes following a 6-Day Plan.

Proceeding into the units, Sydney's group used the 5-Day Plan. Sydney passed Units 1–4 with 100% accuracy. At Unit 5, Sydney received a Pass but had difficulty blending "Dad" smoothly in Subtest C Smooth Blending.

STUDENT ASSESSMENT RECORD

Name: Sydney

UNIT 5	ASSESSMENT ITEMS	SCORE/COMMENTS
Subtest A	M d ee s a D	Goal 5/6 — 6/6
Subtest B	a·m am	Goal 2/2 — 2/2
Subtest C	Seed me add ~~dad~~ (D-ad)	Goal 3/4 — 3/4 Hesitant on the subtest.
Subtest D	Said I	Goal 2/2 — 2/2
Subtest E	"I'm sad. D-ad/SC I see me," said Dad.	Goal 6/7 — 7/7 Slow
Assessment Date(s): 11/03		Goals Met 5/5 Subtests (P) (all subtests) NP

UNIT 6	ASSESSMENT ITEMS	SCORE/COMMENTS
Subtest A	D m e d th A	Goal 5/6 — __/6
Subtest B	D·a·d Dad	Goal 2/2 — __/2
Subtest C	see am add seed	Goal 3/4 — __/4
Subtest D	the I'm said	Goal 3/3 — __/3
Subtest E	I see the [img]. Sam said, "I am mad."	Accuracy Goal 8/9 __/9 words correct ★ Desired Fluency: 20 seconds or less ___ seconds
Assessment Date(s):		Goals Met ___/5 Subtests SP (all subtests with desired fluency) WP (4/5 subtests, and/or fails to attain the desired fluency) NP (fails 2 or more subtests)

134 Blackline Master ★ First Timed Reading ©2008 Sopris West Educational Services. All rights reserved.

SECTION 4: Making Decisions
Group Record Keeping

At Unit 6, Sydney received a Weak Pass because of errors and low fluency. By reviewing the Group Assessment Record, Mrs. Jones noted that Sydney and two others in her group were continuing to have difficulty. Therefore, before proceeding to Unit 7, Mrs. Jones decided to extend group practice in Unit 6. By looking at the Group Assessment Record, Mrs. Jones concluded that the students were doing fine with Sounds and Tricky Words but were having difficulty with Smooth Blending. Mrs. Jones added three Extra Practice lessons at Unit 6 with an increased focus on Smooth Blending of words.

GROUP ASSESSMENT RECORD — UNITS 6–8

Group Name: Mrs. Jones Group 2

Directions
1. For each subtest, write the goal in the appropriate column header. (Subtest goals are located at the bottom of each assessment.)
2. For each student and subtest, record the number of correct responses over the number of possible responses (e.g., 4/5). Circle scores of subtests not passed.
3. For the Sentence Fluency score (last column), record the number of seconds it takes the student to complete the sentence reading. Circle scores that do not meet the desired fluency goal.
4. Using the guide on each Student Assessment Record, determine and record a Strong Pass, Weak Pass, or a No Pass.
5. For students who do not pass, provide additional practice and retest. Record retest scores to the right of the original scores.

Student Names	Unit 6 Date 10/17	Subtest A Sounds Goal 5/6	Subtest B Smooth and Bumpy Blending Goal 2/2	Subtest C Smooth Blending Goal 3/4	Subtest D Tricky Words Goal 3/3	Subtest E Sentences Goal 8/9	Sentence Fluency Goal ≤20 seconds	Unit 7 Date 10/28	Subtest A Sounds Goal 5/6	Subtest B Smooth and Bumpy Blending Goal 2/2	Subtest C Smooth Blending Goal 3/4	Subtest D Tricky Words Goal 3/3	Subtest E Sentences Goal 8/9	Sentence Fluency Goal ≤20 seconds
Miguel	(SP)/WP/NP	6/6	2/2	4/4	3/3	9/9	14	(SP)/WP/NP	6/6	2/2	4/4	3/3	9/9	13
Tom	(SP)/WP/NP	6/6	2/2	3/4	3/3	8/9	19	SP/(WP)/NP	6/6	2/2	2/4	3/3	8/9	21
Tamika	(SP)/WP/NP	6/6	2/2	4/4	3/3	9/9	16	(SP)/WP/NP	6/6	2/2	4/4	3/3	9/9	15
Sydney	SP/(WP)/NP	6/6	1/2	3/4	3/3	8/9	25	(SP)/WP/NP	6/6	2/2	4/4	3/3	9/9	19
Samantha	(SP)/WP/NP	6/6	2/2	3/4	3/3	8/9	20	SP/(WP)/NP	6/6	2/2	3/4	3/3	7/9	20
Eric	(SP)/WP/NP	6/6	2/2	4/4	3/3	9/9	14	(SP)/WP/NP	6/6	2/2	4/4	3/3	9/9	16
Raymond	(SP)/WP/NP	6/6	2/2	4/4	3/3	9/9	13	(SP)/WP/NP	6/6	2/2	4/4	3/3	9/9	15
Rosa	(SP)/WP/NP	6/6	2/2	4/4	3/3	9/9	15	(SP)/WP/NP	6/6	2/2	4/4	3/3	9/9	16

In addition, Mrs. Jones found that Sydney was the weakest student in the group, so she designed a quick individual intervention for Sydney. Mrs. Jones determined, by looking at Sydney's assessments, that the student actually began having difficulty in Unit 5. Sydney had difficulty with Smooth Blending of the word "Dad," the first word with a quick sound at the beginning of the word.

SECTION 4 — Making Decisions
Group Record Keeping

Sydney received a special practice card.

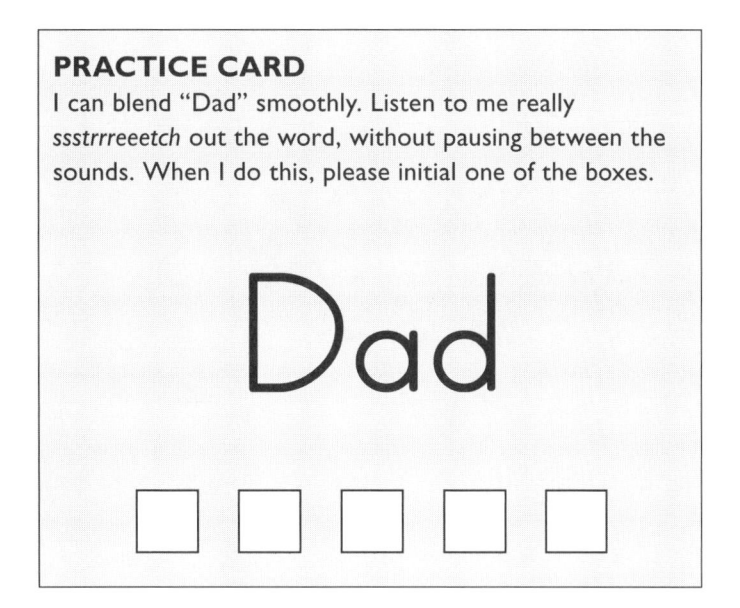

PRACTICE CARD
I can blend "Dad" smoothly. Listen to me really *ssstrrreeetch* out the word, without pausing between the sounds. When I do this, please initial one of the boxes.

Dad

☐ ☐ ☐ ☐ ☐

Sydney carried her special card around during the day. By the end of the day, Mrs. Jones had initialed Sydney's note twice. Mr. Daniels, the instructional assistant, had initialed the note three times.

Each day, Sydney began her day with a special note prepared by Mr. Daniels. Some days, the note included a Smooth Blending word with the letter d. Other days, the note included a sentence for Sydney to read.

At the end of Unit 7, Sydney received a Strong Pass and a certificate for her extra efforts. Mrs. Jones was very pleased but noted that Tom and Samantha continued to earn Weak Passes. Mrs. Jones decided to put Tom and Samantha on the *special card* system. This time, Sydney helped Mrs. Jones and Mr. Daniels initial the notes.

By Unit 8, Tom, Samantha, and Sydney all received Strong Passes.

☺

SECTION 5
Jell-Well Reviews

This section explains how to set up a Jell-Well Review, which takes students back to previous units for a fun review and firming up of knowledge.

Overview and Planning 93

Menu of Prescriptions 99

Jell-Well Planner Blackline Master 104

Children With Special Needs

INSTRUCTIONAL SKILLS

When students struggle, it is important that teachers and support staff receive in-depth training to function as specialists for students at risk of reading difficulties.

Work with your colleagues to determine whether additional training and collaboration would be of benefit. Then seek administrative support. Go to www.ReadWell.net for updates on training and professional development opportunities.

SECTION 5 Jell-Well Reviews

Overview and Planning

What Is a Jell-Well Review?

A Jell-Well Review is the *Read Well* term for a review of earlier units. A Jell-Well Review is a period of time taken to celebrate what children have learned and an opportunity to firm up their foundation of learning.

Why Is a Jell-Well Review Needed?

When children enter school with little or no literacy background, or are among the few children for whom learning to read is extremely difficult, a periodic review of earlier units is sometimes necessary. Without a periodic Jell-Well Review, some children simply become overwhelmed with the process of learning new skills.

When to Do a Jell-Well Review

When a student (or group of students) scores two consecutive Weak Passes or a single No Pass, consider regrouping or implementing a Jell-Well Review. Your discretion is needed. For example, if a student receives a No Pass because of repeated errors on a single word, this student would *not* be a candidate for a Jell-Well Review. This student should proceed with a simple correction of the word. On the other hand, if a student scores two consecutive Weak Passes resulting from a lack of fluency, a quick review of previous units can prevent later difficulties.

SECTION 5 Jell-Well Reviews
Overview and Planning

HOW TO SCHEDULE A JELL-WELL REVIEW

Who...	The Best Option...	When Resources Are Not Available for a Double Dose...
Entire small group	During scheduled instruction and during a second dose of instruction	During scheduled instruction
Part of a group	During a second dose of instruction	Regroup or... Provide part of the group with a short Jell-Well Review during the first 10 minutes of scheduled group lessons.
An individual	During a second dose of instruction	Regroup

How to Plan a Jell-Well Review

Follow the steps below in combination with the directions on the Planner. (See page 104.)

1. **Record assessment results at the top of the Jell-Well Planner.**
   List students with strong assessment results first. Then list students who would benefit from a Jell-Well Review.

2. **Determine where to start the Jell-Well Review.**
   - Find the last unit in which all children received a 100% (Units 1–5) or the last unit in which all children received a Strong Pass (Units 6–20) and start the Jell-Well Review with the next unit.
   - For groups that have mixed skill deficits, go back to the last easy vowel unit. Start the Jell-Well Review there. Skip easy units (usually consonant units). Review all difficult units (usually vowel units). Slow the rate of the review when the skills become more difficult, either by extending the number of days spent on each unit and/or by reviewing all consecutive units.

Jell-Well Planner
For use with Units 1–20

Planning Information Instructor ____Miles____ Group ____Anacondas____ Grade(s) __K__

Last Unit Completed __10__ Last Unit All Students Completed With 100% or a Strong Pass __3__

Assessment Results/Comments

Strong Passes 1–10: Summer, Raven, Henry, Yetty: Try moving up to next group; double dose in interim

Natalie — Strong Passes 1–7, <u>Weak Pass 8</u>, Strong Pass 9 with reteaching, No Pass 10: Has never mastered Smooth Blending

Arnie — Strong Passes 1–3, <u>Weak Pass 4</u>, Weak Pass 5, Weak Pass 6 with reteaching, Weak Pass 7, Weak Pass 8 with preteaching, Weak Pass 9 with preteaching, No Pass 10: Struggles with vowel /ă/ and /ĭ/, says name instead of sound

Matilde — Strong Passes 1–8, <u>Weak Pass 9</u>, Weak Pass 10: Difficulty with words ending in s and blending /tĭ/

George — Strong Passes 1–8, <u>Weak Pass 9</u>, No Pass 10: Absent many days; says /tuh/ and /wuh/—difficulty causing blending problems, calls short /ĭĭĭ/ by the letter name

SECTION 5 — Jell-Well Reviews
Overview and Planning

3. **Plan diagnostically.**

   Analyze the items each student missed or self-corrected on assessments; list error patterns with each student's name. The pinpointed skills provide a guide for instructional emphasis. For the purpose of maintenance and increased fluency, practice should cover all skills in a review unit.

   Some students will be accurate, but not fluent. Fluency is important, as it reflects depth of knowledge. For students who are accurate but dysfluent, practice on easy skills is required to build speed of recognition and increase access to comprehension.

4. **Set up a tentative schedule for review with the number of days planned per unit.**

   - Plan a 1-Day Review for units that introduce easy skills for students (generally, easy consonant sounds).
   - Plan 2- or 3-Day Reviews for units that introduce difficult skills for students (generally, vowels).
   - If more time for review is needed, consider reteaching each unit.

   (*continued*)

   Tentative Jell-Well Review Schedule (Make adjustments as needed.)
   Jell Well Review Schedule: Go back to Unit 4, 2-Day Review on /ăăă/, stress Smooth Blending, Reteach Units 9 and 10.
   Unit 4 (2-Day), Units 5-7 (1-Day), Unit 8 (2-Day), Reteach Units 9-10 (4-Day) = 15 days
   Difficult Skills and Focus: Blending Smoothly, focus on Stretch and Shrink, Smooth and Bumpy Blending, and Sounding Out Smoothly

SECTION 5: Jell-Well Reviews
Overview and Planning

5. Develop lesson plans for each day of the Jell-Well Review.

You can use:

- The review units' Extra Practice lessons, or
- The Jell-Well Review Planner.

Use the review units' Decoding Practices 1–4 (Decoding Practice 4, in particular) as a source for words and word lists.

Use the review units' Solo Stories, Homework, and Extra Practice for repeated reading practice.

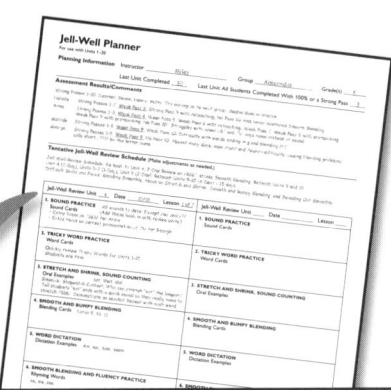

Jell-Well Review Unit __4__ Date __10/18__ Lesson __1 of 2__	Jell-Well Review Unit ____ Date _____ Lesson ____
1. SOUND PRACTICE All sounds to date: Except /w/ and /ĭ/. Sound Cards (Add these back in with review units.) • Extra focus on /ăăă/ for Arnie • Extra focus on correct pronunciation of /t/ for George	**1. SOUND PRACTICE** Sound Cards
2. TRICKY WORD PRACTICE Word Cards Quickly review Tricky Words for Units 1–10. Students are firm.	**2. TRICKY WORD PRACTICE** Word Cards
3. STRETCH AND SHRINK, SOUND COUNTING Oral Examples sat, that, did Gimmick: Stopwatch Contest, Who can stretch "sat" the longest? Tell students "sat" ends with a quick sound so they really need to stretch /ăăă/. Demonstrate as needed. Repeat with each word.	**3. STRETCH AND SHRINK, SOUND COUNTING** Oral Examples
4. SMOOTH AND BUMPY BLENDING Blending Cards Cards 9, 10, 11	**4. SMOOTH AND BUMPY BLENDING** Blending Cards
5. WORD DICTATION Dictation Examples Am, me, Sam, seem	**5. WORD DICTATION** Dictation Examples
6. SMOOTH BLENDING AND FLUENCY PRACTICE Rhyming Words ee, me, see Discrimination Words am, Sam, seem	**6. SMOOTH BLENDING AND FLUENCY PRACTICE** Rhyming Words Discrimination Words
7. STORY READING Unit 4 Solo Stories 2, 4, 6 Motivation: Transparencies with markers, • Guided, then choral, followed by individual turns • Timings	**7. STORY READING**

(See Section 5 of the *Assessment Manual* for ways to vary practice.)

104   Blackline Master   © 2008 Sopris West Educational Services. All rights reserved.

SECTION 5 — Jell-Well Reviews
Overview and Planning

Motivating Students

Your biggest challenge is to keep children excited and motivated. When children feel success is unattainable, they often give up. The following guidelines are important during *all* instruction but are critical when working with high-risk readers.

- **To help children understand that success is possible, set informal and quickly attainable goals.**

    For example, if the children are near mastery on a list of words, set an attainable goal. Say something like:

    > Let's see if you can carefully and correctly read all five words in a row.

- **To keep their attention, provide positive contingent descriptive feedback.**

    Contingent descriptive feedback helps children learn exactly *how* they are meeting your expectations and helps them understand how their actions can help them reach their goals. It clarifies for students what they've done correctly and may point out what they've done incorrectly. (With noncontingent praise, a teacher may say "Good job" even though the students missed a word.) The following script illustrates how to provide contingent descriptive feedback.

    In this example, the students are reading the word list: sat, wind, in, sit, hand. If a student (or students) reads "win" instead of "wind," say something like:

Clarify what the students did right.	You carefully read four words.
Point out what was counterproductive.	But I heard a guess on one word. You forgot to read all the way to the end of the word.
Guide students through a correction.	What was the last sound? (/d/) Sound out the hard word. (/wwwiiinnnd/) Tell me the word. (wind)
Restate the attainable goal.	You figured out the word was *wind*, not *win*. The *wind* blew my hat off. Now let's see if you can read all five words carefully and correctly. (sat, wind, in, sit, hand)
Congratulate students on their accomplishments.	You read all five words correctly!

(continued)

97

SECTION 5 Jell-Well Reviews
Overview and Planning

Motivating Students *(continued)*

- **To help children value their successes, celebrate often.**

    When learning to read is a challenge, children often do not recognize or value their own achievements. Help students learn to recognize and take pride in their accomplishments.

    > You read all five words carefully and correctly! Say "We did it!" **(We did it!)**
    > Now stand up and take a bow. I'm going to clap for you!

- **To make practice fun, use gimmicks, gadgets, and games while keeping response rates high.** (See the menu on pages 99–103.)

    Young children love routines but they can also get mired in uninspired practice. Add a few creative twists to maintain motivation. Luckily, young children respond to teacher enthusiasm. A stopwatch can be used to turn practice into a game. With the right comments, a colored marker can take on special meaning.

    > Wow! You can read *would, could,* and *should.* I'm going to write *would, could,* and *should* for you with my purple marker. You can take the words home and put them on your refrigerator.

SECTION 5 Jell-Well Reviews

Menu of Prescriptions

This list of prescriptions is intended to stimulate your imagination with some fun ways to practice that keep response rates high. A Jell-Well Review will not be productive unless practice focuses on accuracy and then fluency. See *Getting Started: A Guide to Implementation* for additional suggestions.

> **IMPORTANT**
> Keep practice light and fun, but focused. Restructure any gimmick or game that results in fewer responses.

SOUND PRACTICE

Gimmick or Game	Instructional Focus	Procedure
Timed Reading	Increased fluency with sounds	Use Decoding Practice 4, Sound Review. • Set a goal of one sound per second. Establish a pace and have students practice a Timed Reading of the sounds. *Let's see if you can read 30 sounds in 30 seconds.* • Once the goal is reached, increase it. *Yesterday, you read 30 sounds in 30 seconds. Do you think we can read 35 sounds in 30 seconds today?*
Transparencies	Increased attention to difficult sounds by varying the response	Use Decoding Practice 4, Sound Review. • Have each student place a transparency over Decoding Practice 4. • Have students underline any difficult sounds or all vowel sounds. *Everyone, underline /sh/. Now underline /ĭ/ . . .* • Have students practice the underlined sounds in a different rhythm (two times, three times) or type of voice (loud, soft). *Whenever you see an underlined sound, read it two times. Listen to me do the square row: /sh/, /ĭ/-/ĭ/, /r/, /ē/-/ē/, /w/, /k/. Now it's your turn.*
Who Can Hold the Sound the Longest?	Increased accuracy	Use Sound Cards. • Put a paper clip on the difficult sound as a signal. • When the paper-clipped card comes up in Sound Card Practice, practice the sound, then see who can hold the sound the longest without taking a breath. *There's the hard sound. My turn. Listen. /īīī/.* *Your turn. (/īīīīīī/)* *Now let's see who can hold /īīī/ the longest.* *Remember, when you take a breath, you're out.*

(continued)

SECTION 5: Jell-Well Reviews
Menu of Prescriptions

SOUND PRACTICE (continued)

Sticky Notes	Distributed Practice—practice throughout the day	At the end of the lesson, give each child a special sticky note with his or her special sound or Tricky Word written on it. Roberto, you worked hard and learned /ĭĭĭ/ today. I'm going to write your special sound on this sticky note. What sound? (/ĭĭĭ/) Yes, /ĭĭĭ/ as in insect. Put it on your desk. When I go by your desk, you can tell me what it says. If you don't play with it, you can take the note home and keep it.

Prevent guessing. Identify words missed and error patterns. Every time the student reads a Tricky Word incorrectly, he or she is reinforcing an error pattern.

TRICKY WORD PRACTICE

Gimmick or Game	Instructional Focus	Procedure
Don't Let the Tricky Word Fool You!	Increased accuracy	Use Tricky Word Cards. • Identify a difficult word. Write the word (e.g., want) on additional cards. • Put a paper clip on each difficult Tricky Word card as a signal. • Before starting the Tricky Word practice, have students try sounding out the word. Then use the word in a sentence. Our goal is to not let the Tricky Word *want* fool us. Watch for the paper clips. Each paper clip tells us that we need to stop and think, so we don't read the wrong word. Sound out the Tricky Word. (/wwwăăănnnt/) You don't say "I /wănt/ a new pencil." What do you say? (I *want* a new pencil.) Tell me the word. (want) • Take the paper clips off the cards and reset the goal. I'm going to take the paper clips off the Tricky Word *want*. Don't let it fool you. If you aren't sure of a word, stop and sound it out.
Goodbye Tricky Words (chalkboard game)	Increased accuracy and fluency	Put a column of Tricky Words on the board. There should be more than two difficult words. When students master the list, erase each word. First word. (a) Say goodbye *a*. **Erase "a."** Next word. (isn't) Say goodbye *isn't*. **Erase "isn't."** Next word. (wasn't) Say goodbye *wasn't*. **Erase "wasn't."** Next word. (want) Say goodbye *want*. **Erase "want."**

SECTION 5 — Jell-Well Reviews
Menu of Prescriptions

STRETCH AND SHRINK

Gimmick or Game	Instructional Focus	Procedure
Stopwatch Contest, Timed Stretches	Phonemic Awareness—training to facilitate Smooth Blending	• Have fun helping students really *ssstrrrrrreeeeeetch* the words out smoothly. • After practicing, tell students they can play a game to see who can stretch a word the longest. Let's see who can stretch *sad* the longest. It ends with a quick sound so you really need to stretch /sss/ and /ăăă/ a long time. Let's time me first. Listen. /sssssăăăăăd/ That was five seconds. Who can do it even longer? Remember, don't stop between the sounds.

SMOOTH AND BUMPY BLENDING

Gimmick or Game	Instructional Focus	Procedure
Catch the Teacher	Phonemic Awareness—training to facilitate Smooth Blending	• Copy a list of pattern words from a Decoding Practice onto the chalkboard. • Tell students they get to try to catch you doing Bumpy Blending. Listen to me sound out a word. If I do Smooth Blending, give me a thumbs up. If you catch me doing Bumpy Blending, say "Bump, bump, bump!"

Smooth Blending

When children have difficulty blending sounds into words, make sure all adults who are working with children know how to do Smooth Blending.

Word	Correct	Incorrect
am	/ăăămmm/	/ăăă/•/mmm/
see	/sssēēē/	/sss/•/ēēē/
mad	/mmmăăăd/	/mmm/•/ăăăd/ /măăăd/ (/mmm/ is continuous)
did	/dĭĭĭd/	/d/•/ĭĭĭd/ /dĭ/•/d/ (/d/•/ĭ/•/d/)

Provide multiple opportunities for children to do Smooth Blending of words.

SECTION 5: Jell-Well Reviews
Menu of Prescriptions

	ACCURACY AND FLUENCY	
Gimmick or Game	**Instructional Focus**	**Procedure**
Transparencies	Increased accuracy	• Have each student place a transparency over Decoding Practice 4. • Have students underline each letter that changes on a list. • Have students read each underlined letter three times and then read the whole word. • Have students practice the list for fluency. • When the list is mastered by the group and individuals, have students cross out the list, draw happy faces, or draw stars.
Word Charts and Pointers	Increased accuracy and fluency	• Copy lists from the review unit's Decoding Practice onto large flip charts and color code any difficult words. • Have students lead the practice using a pointer with a fun toy on the end (e.g, a plastic fly for Unit 20 with /-y/ as in fly). [Marshall], you were sitting up and paying attention. You get to be the teacher. Here's the pointer. Which column would you like to teach? **As the student points, provide verbal prompts for each response.** Everyone, watch [Marshall's] pointer. First word. (man)

SECTION 5: Jell-Well Reviews

Menu of Prescriptions

Work diagnostically with repeated readings. See *Getting Started: A Guide to Implementation* for a longer list of ways to increase fluency through repeated readings.

	STORY READING	
Gimmick or Game	**Instructional Focus**	**Procedure**
Starred Words One-to-One	Units 1–6 Heavily guided practice (Fluency isn't relevant in the early units, but some students have difficulty getting the sounding out process going as they try to read short sentences.)	Use Homework or Extra Practice passages. • Work one-to-one for a few minutes each day. • Work on one sentence at a time. Start sounding out a word just ahead of the student's normal response rate. Fade your voice as the student sounds out the rest of the word, but lead back in to get the student started on the next word. • Have the student immediately repeat the sentence. Draw a star above each word sounded out without your assistance.
Starred Words, Sentences, or Paragraphs	Accuracy, Units 1–20	Use Homework Stories or Extra Practice passages. • Guide a choral reading of the story. • Provide individual turns while others whisper read and follow each word with their fingers. While an individual reads, draw stars on the student's story directly above *each* word read correctly without guessing or self-correcting. Accept and encourage sounding out. • Provide additional attempts as time allows. (For students in higher units, draw stars at the end of sentences or paragraphs.)

TIP FOR JELL-WELL ACTIVITIES

If children need a Jell-Well Review, it is very important to *not* introduce new words and sounds.

A Jell-Well Review provides young children with a moment to relax, revisit favorite stories, and learn the rewards of mastering skills.

Jell-Well Planner
For use with Units 1–20

Planning Information   Instructor _____   Group _____   Grade(s) _____

Last Unit Completed _____   Last Unit All Students Completed With 100% or a Strong Pass _____

Assessment Results/Comments

Tentative Jell-Well Review Schedule (Make adjustments as needed.)

Jell-Well Review Unit ____ Date _____ Lesson ____	Jell-Well Review Unit ____ Date _____ Lesson ____
1. SOUND PRACTICE Sound Cards	**1. SOUND PRACTICE** Sound Cards
2. TRICKY WORD PRACTICE Word Cards	**2. TRICKY WORD PRACTICE** Word Cards
3. STRETCH AND SHRINK, SOUND COUNTING Oral Examples	**3. STRETCH AND SHRINK, SOUND COUNTING** Oral Examples
4. SMOOTH AND BUMPY BLENDING Blending Cards	**4. SMOOTH AND BUMPY BLENDING** Blending Cards
5. WORD DICTATION Dictation Examples	**5. WORD DICTATION** Dictation Examples
6. SMOOTH BLENDING AND FLUENCY PRACTICE Rhyming Words Discrimination Words	**6. SMOOTH BLENDING AND FLUENCY PRACTICE** Rhyming Words Discrimination Words
7. STORY READING	**7. STORY READING**

(See Section 5 of the *Assessment Manual* for ways to vary practice.)

SECTION 6
Assessments and Forms

This section includes the end-of-unit administration and record keeping forms.

Decoding Assessments, Preludes A–C 106

Decoding Assessments, Units 1–15 109

Oral Reading Fluency Assessments, Units 16–20 124

Decoding Diagnosis, Unit 20 129

Student Assessment Records 130

Group Assessment Records 142

Permission is granted for the purchasing teacher to reproduce these blackline masters for use in his or her classroom only.

PRELUDE A DECODING ASSESSMENT — ADMINISTRATION

SUBTEST A. TRACKING SOUNDS AND PICTURE WORDS GOAL 4/4

Have the student touch and read. Touch the dot under the first sound. Read the sound (or picture word).

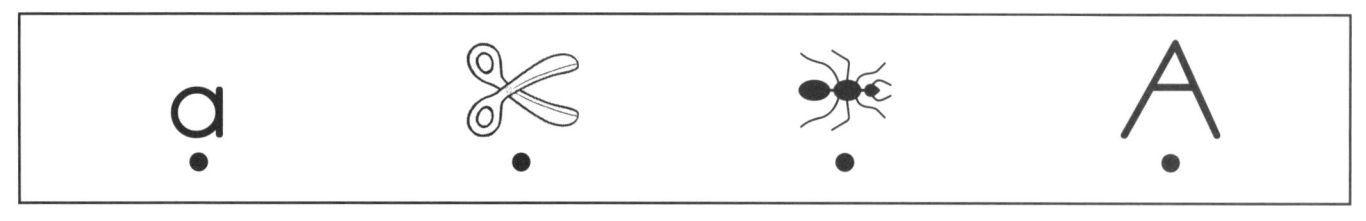

a ✂ 🐜 A

SUBTEST B. COMPREHENSION GOAL 2/2

Read the story to the student. Point to the picture and ask:
Who is this?
What is Anthony doing?

This is Anthony.
Anthony is riding a bike.

SCORING — If the student needs assistance, the item is incorrect.
PASS — The student meets the goals on all subtests. Proceed to Prelude B.
NO PASS — The student fails to meet the goal on 1 or more subtests. Proceed to Prelude A Extra Practice lessons, then retest.

PRELUDE B DECODING ASSESSMENT — ADMINISTRATION

SUBTEST A. TRACKING SOUNDS AND PICTURE WORDS — GOAL 5/5

Have the student touch and read. Touch the dot under the first sound. Read the sound (or picture word).

SUBTEST B. SMOOTH AND BUMPY BLENDING — GOAL 2/2

Have the student touch each square and do Bumpy Blending.
Have the student follow the loop and do Smooth Blending.

SUBTEST C. COMPREHENSION — GOAL 2/2

Read the story to the student. Point to the picture and ask:
Who is the story about?
What are Edith and Ann doing?

Edith and Ann are friends.
Friends sing songs together.
Edith and Ann are singing together.

SCORING	If the student needs assistance, the item is incorrect.
PASS	The student meets the goals on all subtests. Proceed to Prelude C.
NO PASS	The student fails to meet the goal on 1 or more subtests. Proceed to Prelude B Extra Practice lessons, then retest.

©2008 Sopris West Educational Services. All rights reserved.

PRELUDE C DECODING ASSESSMENT — ADMINISTRATION

SUBTEST A. TRACKING SOUNDS AND PICTURE WORDS GOAL 5/5

Have the student touch and read. Touch the dot under the first sound. Read the sound.

a   m   I   A   M

SUBTEST B. SMOOTH AND BUMPY BLENDING GOAL 2/2

Have the student touch each square and do Bumpy Blending.
Have the student follow the loop and do Smooth Blending.

M M M   I'm

SUBTEST C. COMPREHENSION GOAL 2/2

Read the story to the student. Point to the picture and ask:
Who is the story about? What did Farmer Jones want?
Optional: Where does the story take place?

Farmer Jones lived on a farm.
He wanted a dog.

SCORING	If the student needs assistance, the item is incorrect.
PASS	The student meets the goals on all subtests. Proceed to Unit 1.
NO PASS	The student fails to meet the goal on 1 or more subtests. Proceed to Prelude C Extra Practice lessons, then retest.

UNIT 1 DECODING ASSESSMENT — ADMINISTRATION

SUBTEST A. SOUNDS AND WORDS — GOAL 6/6

S m a s M I

SUBTEST B. SMOOTH AND BUMPY BLENDING — GOAL 4/4

sss   sss   aaa   aaa

SUBTEST C. FINGER TRACKING — GOAL 4/4

s   I   S   I

SCORING — If the student needs assistance, the item is incorrect.
PASS — The student meets the goals on all subtests. Proceed to Unit 2.
NO PASS — The student fails to meet the goal on 1 or more subtests. Provide Extra Practice lessons and retest. Consider providing instruction in Preludes A, B, and C. See the *Assessment Manual* for additional information.

©2008 Sopris West Educational Services. All rights reserved.

Blackline Master

UNIT 2 DECODING ASSESSMENT — ADMINISTRATION

SUBTEST A. SOUNDS   GOAL 5/5

m   ee   S   a   e

SUBTEST B. SMOOTH AND BUMPY BLENDING   GOAL 4/4

a a a   aaa   s ee   see

SUBTEST C. TRICKY WORD   GOAL 1/1

I

SUBTEST D. SENTENCE   GOAL 2/2

I see.

SCORING   If the student needs assistance, the item is incorrect.
PASS   The student meets the goals on all subtests. Proceed to Unit 3.
NO PASS   The student fails to meet the goal on 1 or more subtests. Provide Extra Practice lessons and retest. Consider providing instruction in Preludes A, B, and C. See the *Assessment Manual* for additional information.

UNIT 3 DECODING ASSESSMENT — ADMINISTRATION

SUBTEST A. SOUNDS — GOAL 6/6

s ee M e S m

SUBTEST B. SMOOTH AND BUMPY BLENDING — GOAL 4/4

m m m   mmm   m e   me

SUBTEST C. TRICKY WORD (AND I'M) — GOAL 2/2

I   I'm

SUBTEST D. SENTENCE — GOAL 3/3

I see me.

SCORING — If the student needs assistance, the item is incorrect.
PASS — The student meets the goals on all subtests. Proceed to Unit 4.
NO PASS — The student fails to meet the goal on 1 or more subtests. Provide Extra Practice lessons and retest or administer assessments from earlier units to determine where to begin a Jell-Well Review. See the *Assessment Manual*.

©2008 Sopris West Educational Services. All rights reserved.

UNIT 4 DECODING ASSESSMENT — ADMINISTRATION

SUBTEST A. SOUNDS   GOAL 5/6

A m s e M a

SUBTEST B. SMOOTH AND BUMPY BLENDING   GOAL 4/4

a m   am   m e   me

SUBTEST C. TRICKY WORD (AND I'M)   GOAL 2/2

I'm   I

SUBTEST D. SENTENCES   GOAL 6/6

I see me.

I am 🙂.

SCORING	If the student needs assistance, the item is incorrect.
PASS	The student meets the goals on all subtests. Proceed to Unit 5.
NO PASS	The student fails to meet the goal on 1 or more subtests. Provide Extra Practice lessons and retest or administer assessments from earlier units to determine where to begin a Jell-Well Review. See the *Assessment Manual*.

UNIT 5 DECODING ASSESSMENT — ADMINISTRATION

SUBTEST A. SOUNDS — GOAL 5/6

M d ee s a D

SUBTEST B. SMOOTH AND BUMPY BLENDING — GOAL 2/2

a m am

SUBTEST C. SMOOTH BLENDING — GOAL 3/4

Seed me add dad

SUBTEST D. TRICKY WORDS — GOAL 2/2

Said I

SUBTEST E. SENTENCES — GOAL 6/7

"I'm sad.

I see me," said Dad.

SCORING	If the student needs assistance, the item is incorrect.
PASS	The student meets the goals on all subtests. Proceed to Unit 6.
NO PASS	The student fails to meet the goal on 1 or more subtests. Provide Extra Practice lessons and retest or administer assessments from earlier units to determine where to begin a Jell-Well Review. See the *Assessment Manual*.

©2008 Sopris West Educational Services. All rights reserved.

UNIT 6 DECODING ASSESSMENT — ADMINISTRATION

SUBTEST A. SOUNDS — GOAL 5/6

D m e d th A

SUBTEST B. SMOOTH AND BUMPY BLENDING — GOAL 2/2

D a d   Dad

SUBTEST C. SMOOTH BLENDING — GOAL 3/4

see   am   add   seed

SUBTEST D. TRICKY WORDS (AND I'M) — GOAL 3/3

the   I'm   said

SUBTEST E. SENTENCES ★ Desired Fluency: 20 seconds or less — GOAL 8/9

I see the 🐱.

Sam said, "I am mad."

SCORING	If the student needs assistance, the item is incorrect.
STRONG PASS	The student meets the goals on all subtests and has attained the desired fluency. Proceed to Unit 7.
WEAK PASS	The student meets the goals on 4 out of 5 subtests and/or fails to attain the desired fluency. Proceed to Unit 7 with added practice on difficult skills, or provide Extra Practice lessons in Unit 6, and/or provide a Jell-Well Review.
NO PASS	The student fails to meet the goals on 2 or more subtests. Provide Extra Practice lessons and retest, and/or provide a Jell-Well Review.

Blackline Master

©2008 Sopris West Educational Services. All rights reserved.

| UNIT 7 DECODING ASSESSMENT | ADMINISTRATION |

SUBTEST A. SOUNDS — GOAL 5/6

th   ee   n   d   a   N

SUBTEST B. SMOOTH AND BUMPY BLENDING — GOAL 2/2

a n d   and

SUBTEST C. SMOOTH BLENDING — GOAL 3/4

seen   An   than   need

SUBTEST D. TRICKY WORDS (AND I'M) — GOAL 3/3

the   I'm   said

SUBTEST E. SENTENCES   Desired Fluency: 20 seconds or less — GOAL 8/9

I need the 🐕.

I see Dad and Sam.

SCORING	If the student needs assistance, the item is incorrect.
STRONG PASS	The student meets the goals on all subtests and has attained the desired fluency. Proceed to Unit 8.
WEAK PASS	The student meets the goals on 4 out of 5 subtests and/or fails to attain the desired fluency. Proceed to Unit 8 with added practice on difficult skills, or provide Extra Practice lessons in Unit 7, and/or provide a Jell-Well Review.
NO PASS	The student fails to meet the goals on 2 or more subtests. Provide Extra Practice lessons and retest, and/or provide a Jell-Well Review.

©2008 Sopris West Educational Services. All rights reserved.

Blackline Master 115

UNIT 8 DECODING ASSESSMENT — ADMINISTRATION

SUBTEST A. SOUNDS — GOAL 5/6

th a T e N t

SUBTEST B. SMOOTH AND BUMPY BLENDING — GOAL 2/2

Dad   Dad

SUBTEST C. SMOOTH BLENDING — GOAL 3/4

seed   ant   that   Meet

SUBTEST D. TRICKY WORDS — GOAL 3/3

I   the   said

SUBTEST E. SENTENCES   Desired Fluency: 20 seconds or less (21–24 WCPM) — GOAL 7/8

"Meet Sam," said Dad.

I need the man.

SCORING	If the student needs assistance, the item is incorrect.
STRONG PASS	The student meets the goals on all subtests and has attained the desired fluency. Proceed to Unit 9.
WEAK PASS	The student meets the goals on 4 out of 5 subtests and/or fails to attain the desired fluency. Proceed to Unit 9 with added practice on difficult skills, or provide Extra Practice lessons in Unit 8, and/or provide a Jell-Well Review.
NO PASS	The student fails to meet the goals on 2 or more subtests. Provide Extra Practice lessons and retest, and/or provide a Jell-Well Review.

Blackline Master

©2008 Sopris West Educational Services. All rights reserved.

UNIT 9 DECODING ASSESSMENT   ADMINISTRATION

SUBTEST A. SOUNDS   GOAL 5/6

> a   t   ee   M   W   n

SUBTEST B. SMOOTH BLENDING   GOAL 3/4

> we   sat   Than   Meet

SUBTEST C. TRICKY WORDS   GOAL 3/3

> Said   the   was

SUBTEST D. SENTENCES   Desired Fluency: 25 seconds or less (22–24 WCPM)   GOAL 9/10

> Dad said, "See the weeds."
>
> We see that sad man.

SCORING   If the student needs assistance, the item is incorrect.
STRONG PASS   The student meets the goals on all subtests and has attained the desired fluency. Proceed to Unit 10.
WEAK PASS   The student meets the goals on 3 out of 4 subtests and/or fails to attain the desired fluency. Proceed to Unit 10 with added practice on difficult skills, or provide Extra Practice lessons in Unit 9, and/or provide a Jell-Well Review.
NO PASS   The student fails to meet the goals on 2 or more subtests. Provide Extra Practice lessons and retest, and/or provide a Jell-Well Review.

©2008 Sopris West Educational Services. All rights reserved.   Blackline Master

UNIT 10 DECODING ASSESSMENT — ADMINISTRATION

SUBTEST A. SOUNDS   GOAL 5/6

| e   th   N   a   i   w |

SUBTEST B. SMOOTH BLENDING   GOAL 3/4

| it   than   We   dad |

SUBTEST C. TRICKY WORDS   GOAL 3/3

| said   was   Sees |

SUBTEST D. SENTENCES   Desired Fluency: 30 seconds or less (22–24 WCPM)   GOAL 11/12

"I see this seed," said Dad.

Did Tim sit in the sand?

SCORING   If the student needs assistance, the item is incorrect.

STRONG PASS   The student meets the goals on all subtests and has attained the desired fluency. Proceed to Unit 11.

WEAK PASS   The student meets the goals on 3 out of 4 subtests and/or fails to attain the desired fluency. Proceed to Unit 11 with added practice on difficult skills, or provide Extra Practice lessons in Unit 10, and/or provide a Jell-Well Review.

NO PASS   The student fails to meet the goals on 2 or more subtests. Provide Extra Practice lessons and retest, and/or provide a Jell-Well Review.

UNIT 11 DECODING ASSESSMENT — ADMINISTRATION

SUBTEST A. SOUNDS — GOAL 6/7

a   H   d   ee   W   i   h

SUBTEST B. SMOOTH BLENDING — GOAL 4/5

him   had   did   it   swim

SUBTEST C. TRICKY WORDS — GOAL 3/4

is   Was   His   the

SUBTEST D. SENTENCES   Desired Fluency: 30 seconds or less (24–26 WCPM) — GOAL 12/13

He said, "That man is sad."

"Dad sits in the weeds," said Tim.

SCORING   If the student needs assistance, the item is incorrect.
STRONG PASS   The student meets the goals on all subtests and has attained the desired fluency. Proceed to Unit 12.
WEAK PASS   The student meets the goals on 3 out of 4 subtests and/or fails to attain the desired fluency. Proceed to Unit 12 with added practice on difficult skills, or provide Extra Practice lessons in Unit 11, and/or provide a Jell-Well Review.
NO PASS   The student fails to meet the goals on 2 or more subtests. Provide Extra Practice lessons and retest, and/or provide a Jell-Well Review.

©2008 Sopris West Educational Services. All rights reserved.

Blackline Master

UNIT 12 DECODING ASSESSMENT **ADMINISTRATION**

SUBTEST A. SOUNDS GOAL 6/7

C   i   h   e   c   H   N

SUBTEST B. SMOOTH BLENDING GOAL 4/5

had   him   wind   Did   can

SUBTEST C. TRICKY WORDS GOAL 3/4

Wasn't   a   isn't   is

SUBTEST D. SENTENCES Desired Fluency: 30 seconds or less (26–28 WCPM) GOAL 13/14

"He can hit it," said Tim.

He swims with his dad.

I see ants.

SCORING	If the student needs assistance, the item is incorrect.
STRONG PASS	The student meets the goals on all subtests and has attained the desired fluency. Proceed to Unit 13.
WEAK PASS	The student meets the goals on 3 out of 4 subtests and/or fails to attain the desired fluency. Proceed to Unit 13 with added practice on difficult skills, or provide Extra Practice lessons in Unit 12, and/or provide a Jell-Well Review.
NO PASS	The student fails to meet the goals on 2 or more subtests. Provide Extra Practice lessons and retest, and/or provide a Jell-Well Review.

Blackline Master

©2008 Sopris West Educational Services. All rights reserved.

UNIT 13 DECODING ASSESSMENT   ADMINISTRATION

SUBTEST A. SOUNDS   GOAL 6/7

| ea | R | h | d | a | C | r |

SUBTEST B. SMOOTH BLENDING   GOAL 4/5

| hiss | sweet | hit | Can | ran |

SUBTEST C. TRICKY WORDS   GOAL 3/4

| With | want | wasn't | a |

SUBTEST D. SENTENCES   Desired Fluency: 30 seconds or less (28–30 WCPM)   GOAL 14/15

The cat was in the tree.

Three rats hid.

The cat can't see the rats.

SCORING	If the student needs assistance, the item is incorrect.
STRONG PASS	The student meets the goals on all subtests and has attained the desired fluency. Proceed to Unit 14.
WEAK PASS	The student meets the goals on 3 out of 4 subtests and/or fails to attain the desired fluency. Proceed to Unit 14 with added practice on difficult skills, or provide Extra Practice lessons in Unit 13, and/or provide a Jell-Well Review.
NO PASS	The student fails to meet the goals on 2 or more subtests. Provide Extra Practice lessons and retest, and/or provide a Jell-Well Review.

©2008 Sopris West Educational Services. All rights reserved.   Blackline Master   121

UNIT 14 DECODING ASSESSMENT — ADMINISTRATION

SUBTEST A. SOUNDS GOAL 6/7

c   H   e   r   i   w   Sh

SUBTEST B. SMOOTH BLENDING GOAL 4/5

she   Tad   can   dash   read

SUBTEST C. TRICKY WORDS GOAL 3/4

would   with   Want   wasn't

SUBTEST D. SENTENCES   Desired Fluency: 30 seconds or less (30–32 WCPM) GOAL 15/16

She should swim in the sea. I wish we could eat seeds with Dean and Sam.

SCORING	If the student needs assistance, the item is incorrect.
STRONG PASS	The student meets the goals on all subtests and has attained the desired fluency. Proceed to Unit 15.
WEAK PASS	The student meets the goals on 3 out of 4 subtests and/or fails to attain the desired fluency. Proceed to Unit 15 with added practice on difficult skills, or provide Extra Practice lessons in Unit 14, and/or provide a Jell-Well Review.
NO PASS	The student fails to meet the goals on 2 or more subtests. Provide Extra Practice lessons and retest, and/or provide a Jell-Well Review.

UNIT 15 DECODING ASSESSMENT — ADMINISTRATION

SUBTEST A. SOUNDS — GOAL 6/7

R   ck   i   ea   sh   a   K

SUBTEST B. SMOOTH BLENDING — GOAL 4/5

ink   Cass   mean   dish   can't

SUBTEST C. TRICKY WORDS — GOAL 4/5

should   his   a   wasn't   isn't

SUBTEST D. SENTENCES   Desired Fluency: 30 seconds or less (34–36 WCPM) — GOAL 17/18

"Kim was sick that week," said Rick.

I wish she could kick.

"This isn't a trick," said Kim.

SCORING If the student needs assistance, the item is incorrect.
STRONG PASS The student meets the goals on all subtests and has attained the desired fluency. Proceed to Unit 16.
WEAK PASS The student meets the goals on 3 out of 4 subtests and/or fails to attain the desired fluency. Proceed to Unit 16 with added practice on difficult skills, or provide Extra Practice lessons in Unit 15, and/or provide a Jell-Well Review.
NO PASS The student fails to meet the goals on 2 or more subtests. Provide Extra Practice lessons and retest, and/or provide a Jell-Well Review.

©2008 Sopris West Educational Services. All rights reserved.   Blackline Master   123

UNIT 16 ORAL READING FLUENCY ASSESSMENT — ADMINISTRATION

TRICKY WORD WARM-UP

| was | said | into | do | want |

ORAL READING FLUENCY PASSAGE

The Moon

★At noon, Rick can't see the moon. 7
Is the moon in the trash can? 14
Is it in the shack? 19
"I miss the moon," said Kim. 25

ORAL READING FLUENCY	Start timing at the ★. Mark errors. Make a single slash in the text (/) at 60 seconds. Have students complete the passage. If the student completes the passage in less than 60 seconds, have the student go back to the ★ and continue reading. Make a double slash (//) in the text at 60 seconds.
WCPM	Determine words correct per minute by subtracting errors from words read in 60 seconds.
STRONG PASS	The student scores no more than 2 errors on the first pass through the passage and reads a minimum of 36 words correct per minute. Proceed to Unit 17.
WEAK PASS	The student scores no more than 2 errors on the first pass through the passage and reads 28 to 35 words correct per minute. Proceed to Unit 17 with added fluency practice, or provide Extra Practice lessons in Unit 16, and/or provide a Jell-Well Review.
NO PASS	The student scores 3 or more errors on the first pass through the passage and/or reads 27 or fewer words correct per minute. Provide Extra Practice lessons and retest, and/or provide a Jell-Well Review.

UNIT 17 ORAL READING FLUENCY ASSESSMENT — ADMINISTRATION

TRICKY WORD WARM-UP

| Are | want | into | could | do |

ORAL READING FLUENCY PASSAGE

Stars

★Mark said, "It is hard to see the stars." 9

Nan said, "We should see a star. 16

I wish we could." 20

"I think I see three!" said Sid. 27

ORAL READING FLUENCY	Start timing at the ★. Mark errors. Make a single slash in the text (/) at 60 seconds. Have students complete the passage. If the student completes the passage in less than 60 seconds, have the student go back to the ★ and continue reading. Make a double slash (//) in the text at 60 seconds.
WCPM	Determine words correct per minute by subtracting errors from words read in 60 seconds.
STRONG PASS	The student scores no more than 2 errors on the first pass through the passage and reads a minimum of 39 words correct per minute. Proceed to Unit 18.
WEAK PASS	The student scores no more than 2 errors on the first pass through the passage and reads 30 to 38 words correct per minute. Proceed to Unit 18 with added fluency practice, or provide Extra Practice lessons in Unit 17, and/or provide a Jell-Well Review.
NO PASS	The student scores 3 or more errors on the first pass through the passage and/or reads 29 or fewer words correct per minute. Provide Extra Practice lessons and retest, and/or provide a Jell-Well Review.

©2008 Sopris West Educational Services. All rights reserved.   Blackline Master

UNIT 18 ORAL READING FLUENCY ASSESSMENT — ADMINISTRATION

TRICKY WORD WARM-UP

| has | What | should | would | want |

ORAL READING FLUENCY PASSAGE

The Smart Shark

★ What do I see? — 4

I see the shark in the dark sea. — 12

What can that shark do? — 17

He can swim in the sea. — 23

He is a smart shark. — 28

ORAL READING FLUENCY — Start timing at the ★. Mark errors. Make a single slash in the text (/) at 60 seconds. Have students complete the passage. If the student completes the passage in less than 60 seconds, have the student go back to the ★ and continue reading. Make a double slash (//) in the text at 60 seconds.

WCPM — Determine words correct per minute by subtracting errors from words read in 60 seconds.

STRONG PASS — The student scores no more than 2 errors on the first pass through the passage and reads a minimum of 42 words correct per minute. Proceed to Unit 19.

WEAK PASS — The student scores no more than 2 errors on the first pass through the passage and reads 32 to 41 words correct per minute. Proceed to Unit 19 with added fluency practice, or provide Extra Practice lessons in Unit 18, and/or provide a Jell-Well Review.

NO PASS — The student scores 3 or more errors on the first pass through the passage and/or reads 31 or fewer words correct per minute. Provide Extra Practice lessons and retest, and/or provide a Jell-Well Review.

UNIT 19 ORAL READING FLUENCY ASSESSMENT — ADMINISTRATION

TRICKY WORD WARM-UP

| there | what | his | Want | are |

ORAL READING FLUENCY PASSAGE

A Snack

☆ The red hen met the kitten near the shed. — 9

"I want a snack soon," said the red hen. — 18

"Me too," said the kitten. — 23

"We could eat in the car." — 29

ORAL READING FLUENCY — Start timing at the ☆. Mark errors. Make a single slash in the text (/) at 60 seconds. Have students complete the passage. If the student completes the passage in less than 60 seconds, have the student go back to the ☆ and continue reading. Make a double slash (//) in the text at 60 seconds.

WCPM — Determine words correct per minute by subtracting errors from words read in 60 seconds.

STRONG PASS — The student scores no more than 2 errors on the first pass through the passage and reads a minimum of 44 words correct per minute. Proceed to Unit 20.

WEAK PASS — The student scores no more than 2 errors on the first pass through the passage and reads 34 to 43 words correct per minute. Proceed to Unit 20 with added fluency practice, or provide Extra Practice lessons in Unit 19, and/or provide a Jell-Well Review.

NO PASS — The student scores 3 or more errors on the first pass through the passage and/or reads 33 or fewer words correct per minute. Provide Extra Practice lessons and retest, and/or provide a Jell-Well Review.

©2008 Sopris West Educational Services. All rights reserved.

Blackline Master

UNIT 20 ORAL READING FLUENCY ASSESSMENT — ADMINISTRATION

TRICKY WORD WARM-UP

| A | who | What | there | are |

ORAL READING FLUENCY PASSAGE

The Tan Kitten

★Dad said, "I had three little cats." — 7

The tan kitten sat still. — 12

Then she went into the work room. — 19

What did she do there? — 24

Why was she there? — 28

She had a snack. — 32

ORAL READING FLUENCY	Start timing at the ★. Mark errors. Make a single slash in the text (/) at 60 seconds. Have students complete the passage. If the student completes the passage in less than 60 seconds, have the student go back to the ★ and continue reading. Make a double slash (//) in the text at 60 seconds.
WCPM	Determine words correct per minute by subtracting errors from words read in 60 seconds.
STRONG PASS	The student scores no more than 2 errors on the first pass through the passage and reads a minimum of 46 words correct per minute. Assess for placement in *Read Well 1*. Begin with the *Read Well 1* Unit 15 Assessment. Then follow the *Read Well 1* assessment guidelines to determine the next placement step.
WEAK PASS	The student scores no more than 2 errors on the first pass through the passage and reads 36 to 45 words correct per minute. Provide a Jell-Well Review using Extra Practice lessons.
NO PASS	The student scores 3 or more errors on the first pass through the passage and/or reads 35 or fewer words correct per minute. Provide a Jell-Well Review. Administer earlier assessments to determine where the student can earn a Strong Pass. Begin a Jell-Well Review at that unit.

Blackline Master ©2008 Sopris West Educational Services. All rights reserved.

UNIT 20 DECODING DIAGNOSIS — ADMINISTRATION

SOUNDS

ĕ	Th	r	k	oo	E	ar	wh
i	sh	ee	Wh	a	ĕ	H	ea

VOWEL DISCRIMINATION

set	sat	sit	seat
Mark	Mick	Mack	meek

BEGINNING QUICK SOUNDS

dent	hand	test	dark
hit	tent	Kim	dash

BLENDS AND WORD ENDINGS

Trish	snack	creek	kitten
scoot	wham	drink	scat

TRICKY WORDS

where	into	as	wouldn't
what	to	There	are

- Have students read from a clean copy of the Decoding Diagnosis. Record incorrect responses on another copy.
- Use information from both the Unit 20 Fluency Assessment and the Unit 20 Decoding Diagnosis to identify specific skill deficits.

©2008 Sopris West Educational Services. All rights reserved.

Blackline Master 129

STUDENT ASSESSMENT RECORD

Name _____ Teacher _____

IMPORTANT: Follow the scoring and recording procedures shown on pages ___ (Preludes A–C and Units 1–15) and ___ (Units 16–20). For each unit, circle the appropriate pass level: SP (Strong Pass), P (Pass), WP (Weak Pass), or NP (No Pass).

PRELUDE A	ASSESSMENT ITEMS	SCORE/COMMENTS
Subtest A	a ✂ 🐜 A	Goal 4/4 ____/4 The student is able to track. Yes __ No__
Subtest B	Who is this? (This is Anthony.) What is Anthony doing? (Anthony is riding a bike.)	Goal 2/2 ____/2
Assessment Date(s):		Goals Met ____/2 Subtests P (all subtests; proceed to Prelude B) NP (Proceed to Prelude A Extra Practice Lessons, then retest.)

PRELUDE B	ASSESSMENT ITEMS	SCORE/COMMENTS
Subtest A	A 👦 I 👧 m	Goal 5/5 ____/5 The student is able to track. Yes __ No__
Subtest B	Who is the story about? (The story is about Edith and Ann.) What are Edith and Ann doing? (Edith and Ann are singing together.)	Goal 2/2 ____/2
Assessment Date(s):		Goals Met ____/2 Subtests P (all subtests; proceed to Prelude C) NP (Proceed to Prelude B Extra Practice Lesson, then retest.)

STUDENT ASSESSMENT RECORD

Name _____

PRELUDE C	ASSESSMENT ITEMS	SCORE/COMMENTS
Subtest A	a m I A M	Goal 5/5 ____/5 The student is able to track. Yes __ No__
Subtest B	M•M•M I'm	Goal 2/2 ____/2
Subtest C	Who is the story about? (The story is about Farmer Jones.) What did Farmer Jones want? (Farmer Jones wanted a dog.) *Optional:* Where does the story take place? (The story takes place on a farm.)	Goal 2/2 ____/2
Assessment Date(s):		Goals Met ____/3 Subtests **P** (all subtests; proceed to Unit 1) **NP** (Proceed to Prelude C Extra Practice Lesson, then retest.)

©2008 Sopris West Educational Services. All rights reserved.

Blackline Master

STUDENT ASSESSMENT RECORD

Name _____

UNIT 1	ASSESSMENT ITEMS	SCORE/COMMENTS
Subtest A	S m a s M I	Goal 6/6 ____/6
Subtest B	s·s·s sss a·a·a aaa	Goal 4/4 ____/4
Subtest C	s I S I	Goal 4/4 ____/4
Assessment Date(s):		Goals Met ____/3 Subtests P (all subtests) NP

UNIT 2	ASSESSMENT ITEMS	SCORE/COMMENTS
Subtest A	m ee S a e	Goal 5/5 ____/5
Subtest B	a·a·a aaa s·ee see	Goal 4/4 ____/4
Subtest C	I	Goal 1/1 ____/1
Subtest D	I see.	Goal 2/2 ____/2
Assessment Date(s):		Goals Met ____/4 Subtests P (all subtests) NP

STUDENT ASSESSMENT RECORD

Name _____

UNIT 3	ASSESSMENT ITEMS	SCORE/COMMENTS
Subtest A	s ee M e S m	Goal 6/6 ____/6
Subtest B	m·m·m mmm m·e me	Goal 4/4 ____/4
Subtest C	I I'm	Goal 2/2 ____/2
Subtest D	I see me.	Goal 3/3 ____/3
Assessment Date(s):		Goals Met ____/4 Subtests P (all subtests) NP

UNIT 4	ASSESSMENT ITEMS	SCORE/COMMENTS
Subtest A	A m s e M a	Goal 5/6 ____/6
Subtest B	a·m am m·e me	Goal 4/4 ____/4
Subtest C	I'm I	Goal 2/2 ____/2
Subtest D	I see me. I am 🙂.	Goal 6/6 ____/6
Assessment Date(s):		Goals Met ____/4 Subtests P (all subtests) NP

STUDENT ASSESSMENT RECORD

Name _____

UNIT 5	ASSESSMENT ITEMS	SCORE/COMMENTS
Subtest A	M d ee s a D	Goal 5/6 ____/6
Subtest B	a·m am	Goal 2/2 ____/2
Subtest C	Seed me add dad	Goal 3/4 ____/4
Subtest D	Said I	Goal 2/2 ____/2
Subtest E	"I'm sad. I see me," said Dad.	Goal 6/7 ____/7
Assessment Date(s):		Goals Met ____/5 Subtests P (all subtests) NP

UNIT 6	ASSESSMENT ITEMS	SCORE/COMMENTS
Subtest A	D m e d th A	Goal 5/6 ____/6
Subtest B	D·a·d Dad	Goal 2/2 ____/2
Subtest C	see am add seed	Goal 3/4 ____/4
Subtest D	the I'm said	Goal 3/3 ____/3
Subtest E	I see the [image]. Sam said, "I am mad."	Accuracy Goal 8/9 ____/9 words correct ★ Desired Fluency: 20 seconds or less ____ seconds
Assessment Date(s):		Goals Met ____/5 Subtests SP (all subtests with desired fluency) WP (4/5 subtests, and/or fails to attain the desired fluency) NP (fails 2 or more subtests)

STUDENT ASSESSMENT RECORD

Name _____

UNIT 7	ASSESSMENT ITEMS	SCORE/COMMENTS
Subtest A	th ee n d a N	Goal 5/6 ____/6
Subtest B	a·n·d and	Goal 2/2 ____/2
Subtest C	seen An than need	Goal 3/4 ____/4
Subtest D	the I'm said	Goal 3/3 ____/3
Subtest E	I need the 🐕. I see Dad and Sam.	Accuracy Goal 8/9 ____/9 words correct Desired Fluency: 20 seconds or less ____ seconds
Assessment Date(s):		Goals Met ____/5 Subtests SP (all subtests with desired fluency) WP (4/5 subtests, and/or fails to attain the desired fluency) NP (fails 2 or more subtests)

UNIT 8	ASSESSMENT ITEMS	SCORE/COMMENTS
Subtest A	th a T e N t	Goal 5/6 ____/6
Subtest B	D·a·d Dad	Goal 2/2 ____/2
Subtest C	Seed ant that Meet	Goal 3/4 ____/4
Subtest D	I the said	Goal 3/3 ____/3
Subtest E	"Meet Sam," said Dad. I need the man.	Accuracy Goal 7/8 ____/8 words correct Desired Fluency: 20 seconds or less (21–24 WCPM) ____ seconds
Assessment Date(s):		Goals Met ____/5 Subtests SP (all subtests with desired fluency) WP (4/5 subtests, and/or fails to attain the desired fluency) NP (fails 2 or more subtests)

©2008 Sopris West Educational Services. All rights reserved.   Blackline Master

STUDENT ASSESSMENT RECORD

Name _____

UNIT 9	ASSESSMENT ITEMS	SCORE/COMMENTS
Subtest A	a t ee M W n	Goal 5/6 ____/6
Subtest B	we sat Than Meet	Goal 3/4 ____/4
Subtest C	Said the was	Goal 3/3 ____/3
Subtest D	Dad said, "See the weeds." We see that sad man.	Accuracy Goal 9/10 ____/10 words correct Desired Fluency: 25 seconds or less (22–24 WCPM) ____ seconds
Assessment Date(s):		Goals Met ____/4 Subtests SP (all subtests with desired fluency) WP (3/4 subtests, and/or fails to attain the desired fluency) NP (fails 2 or more subtests)

UNIT 10	ASSESSMENT ITEMS	SCORE/COMMENTS
Subtest A	e th N a i w	Goal 5/6 ____/6
Subtest B	it than We dad	Goal 3/4 ____/4
Subtest C	said was Sees	Goal 3/3 ____/3
Subtest D	"I see this seed," said Dad. Did Tim sit in the sand?	Accuracy Goal 11/12 ____/12 words correct Desired Fluency: 30 seconds or less (22–24 WCPM) ____ seconds
Assessment Date(s):		Goals Met ____/4 Subtests SP (all subtests with desired fluency) WP (3/4 subtests, and/or fails to attain the desired fluency) NP (fails 2 or more subtests)

Blackline Master   ©2008 Sopris West Educational Services. All rights reserved.

STUDENT ASSESSMENT RECORD

Name _____

UNIT 11	ASSESSMENT ITEMS	SCORE/COMMENTS
Subtest A	a H d ee W i h	Goal 6/7 ____/7
Subtest B	him had did it swim	Goal 4/5 ____/5
Subtest C	is Was His the	Goal 3/4 ____/4
Subtest D	He said, "That man is sad." "Dad sits in the weeds," said Tim.	Accuracy Goal 12/13 ____/13 words correct Desired Fluency: 30 seconds or less (24–26 WCPM) ____ seconds
Assessment Date(s):		Goals Met ____/4 Subtests **SP** (all subtests with desired fluency) **WP** (3/4 subtests, and/or fails to attain the desired fluency) **NP** (fails 2 or more subtests)

UNIT 12	ASSESSMENT ITEMS	SCORE/COMMENTS
Subtest A	C i h e c H N	Goal 6/7 ____/7
Subtest B	had him wind Did can	Goal 4/5 ____/5
Subtest C	Wasn't a isn't is	Goal 3/4 ____/4
Subtest D	"He can hit it," said Tim. He swims with his dad. I see ants.	Accuracy Goal 13/14 ____/14 words correct Desired Fluency: 30 seconds or less (26–28 WCPM) ____ seconds
Assessment Date(s):		Goals Met ____/4 Subtests **SP** (all subtests with desired fluency) **WP** (3/4 subtests, and/or fails to attain the desired fluency) **NP** (fails 2 or more subtests)

©2008 Sopris West Educational Services. All rights reserved.

Blackline Master

STUDENT ASSESSMENT RECORD

Name _____

UNIT 13	ASSESSMENT ITEMS	SCORE/COMMENTS
Subtest A	ea R h d a C r	Goal 6/7 ____/7
Subtest B	hiss sweet hit Can ran	Goal 4/5 ____/5
Subtest C	With want wasn't a	Goal 3/4 ____/4
Subtest D	The cat was in the tree. Three rats hid. The cat can't see the rats.	Accuracy Goal 14/15 ____/15 words correct Desired Fluency: 30 seconds or less (28–30 WCPM) ____ seconds
Assessment Date(s):		Goals Met ____/4 Subtests **SP** (all subtests with desired fluency) **WP** (3/4 subtests, and/or fails to attain the desired fluency) **NP** (fails 2 or more subtests)

UNIT 14	ASSESSMENT ITEMS	SCORE/COMMENTS
Subtest A	c H e r i w Sh	Goal 6/7 ____/7
Subtest B	she Tad can dash read	Goal 4/5 ____/5
Subtest C	would with Want wasn't	Goal 3/4 ____/4
Subtest D	She should swim in the sea. I wish we could eat seeds with Dean and Sam.	Accuracy Goal 15/16 ____/16 words correct Desired Fluency: 30 seconds or less (30–32 WCPM) ____ seconds
Assessment Date(s):		Goals Met ____/4 Subtests **SP** (all subtests with desired fluency) **WP** (3/4 subtests, and/or fails to attain the desired fluency) **NP** (fails 2 or more subtests)

138 Blackline Master   ©2008 Sopris West Educational Services. All rights reserved.

STUDENT ASSESSMENT RECORD

Name _____

UNIT 15	ASSESSMENT ITEMS	SCORE/COMMENTS
Subtest A	R　ck　i　ea　sh　a　K	Goal 6/7 ____/7
Subtest B	ink　Cass　mean　dish　can't	Goal 4/5 ____/5
Subtest C	should　his　a　wasn't　isn't	Goal 4/5 ____/5
Subtest D	"Kim was sick that week," said Rick. I wish she could kick. "This isn't a trick," said Kim.	Accuracy Goal 17/18 ____/18 words correct Desired Fluency: 30 seconds or less (34–36 WCPM) ____ seconds
Assessment Date(s):		Goals Met ____/4 Subtests SP (all subtests with desired fluency) WP (3/4 subtests, and/or fails to attain the desired fluency) NP (fails 2 or more subtests)

UNIT 16	ASSESSMENT ITEMS	SCORE/COMMENTS
Tricky Word Warm-Up	was　said　into　do　want	
Oral Reading Fluency Passage	The Moon ★At noon, Rick can't see the moon.　　7 　Is the moon in the trash can?　　14 　Is it in the shack?　　19 　"I miss the moon," said Kim.　　25	Accuracy: ____ Passage Errors Desired Fluency: 36+ words correct per minute **Fluency:** ____ WCPM (____ words read minus ____ errors in one minute)
Assessment Date(s):		SP (no more than 2 errors and 36 or more words correct per minute) WP (no more than 2 errors and 28 to 35 words correct per minute) NP (3 or more errors and/or 27 or fewer words correct per minute)

©2008 Sopris West Educational Services. All rights reserved.

Blackline Master 139

STUDENT ASSESSMENT RECORD

Name _____

UNIT 17	ASSESSMENT ITEMS	SCORE/COMMENTS
Tricky Word Warm-Up	Are want into could do	
Oral Reading Fluency Passage	Stars ★Mark said, "It's hard to see the stars." 9 Nan said, "We should see a star. 16 I wish we could." 19 "I think I see three!" said Sid. 25	Accuracy: ____ Passage Errors Desired Fluency: 39+ words correct per minute **Fluency:** ____ **WCPM** (____ words read minus ____ errors in one minute)
Assessment Date(s):	**SP** (no more than 2 errors and 39 or more words correct per minute) **WP** (no more than 2 errors and 30 to 38 words correct per minute) **NP** (3 or more errors and/or 29 or fewer words correct per minute)	

UNIT 18	ASSESSMENT ITEMS	SCORE/COMMENTS
Tricky Word Warm-Up	has What should would want	
Oral Reading Fluency Passage	The Smart Shark ★What do I see? 4 I see the shark in the dark sea. 12 What can that shark do? 17 He can swim in the sea. 23 He is a smart shark. 28	Accuracy: ____ Passage Errors Desired Fluency: 42+ words correct per minute **Fluency:** ____ **WCPM** (____ words read minus ____ errors in one minute)
Assessment Date(s):	**SP** (no more than 2 errors and 42 or more words correct per minute) **WP** (no more than 2 errors and 32 to 41 words correct per minute) **NP** (3 or more errors and/or 31 or fewer words correct per minute)	

STUDENT ASSESSMENT RECORD

Name _____

UNIT 19	ASSESSMENT ITEMS	SCORE/COMMENTS
Tricky Word Warm-Up	there what his Want are	
Oral Reading Fluency Passage	**A Snack** ★The red hen met the kitten near the shed. 9 "I want a snack soon," said the red hen. 18 "Me too," said the kitten. 23 "We could eat in the car." 29	**Accuracy:** ____ Passage Errors Desired Fluency: 44+ words correct per minute **Fluency:** ____ **WCPM** (____ words read minus ____ errors in one minute)
Assessment Date(s):	SP (no more than 2 errors and 44 or more words correct per minute) WP (no more than 2 errors and 34 to 43 words correct per minute) NP (3 or more errors and/or 33 or fewer words correct per minute)	

UNIT 20	ASSESSMENT ITEMS	SCORE/COMMENTS
Tricky Word Warm-Up	A who What there are	
Oral Reading Fluency Passage	**The Tan Kitten** ★Dad said, "I had three little cats." 7 The tan kitten sat still. 12 Then she went into the work room. 19 What did she do there? 24 Why was she there? 28 She had a snack. 32	**Accuracy:** ____ Passage Errors Desired Fluency: 46+ words correct per minute **Fluency:** ____ **WCPM** (____ words read minus ____ errors in one minute)
Assessment Date(s):	SP (no more than 2 errors and 46 or more words correct per minute) WP (no more than 2 errors and 36 to 45 words correct per minute) NP (3 or more errors and/or 35 or fewer words correct per minute)	

GROUP ASSESSMENT RECORD

PRELUDE A

Directions

1. For each subtest, write the goal in the appropriate column header. (Subtest goals are located at the bottom of each assessment.)
2. For each student and subtest, record the number of correct responses over the number of possible responses (e.g., 4/5). Circle scores of subtests not passed.
3. Using the guide on each Student Assessment Record, determine and record a Pass or a No Pass.
4. For students who do not pass, provide additional practice and retest. Record retest scores to the right of the original scores.

Group Name _____

Student Names	Prelude Date ___	Subtest A Tracking Sounds and Picture Words Goal __/__	Subtest B Comprehension Goal __/__	Prelude Date ___	Subtest A Tracking Sounds and Picture Words Goal __/__	Subtest B Comprehension Goal __/__
	P / NP			P / NP		
	P / NP			P / NP		
	P / NP			P / NP		
	P / NP			P / NP		
	P / NP			P / NP		
	P / NP			P / NP		
	P / NP			P / NP		
	P / NP			P / NP		
	P / NP			P / NP		
	P / NP			P / NP		
	P / NP			P / NP		

Blackline Master

©2008 Sopris West Educational Services. All rights reserved.

GROUP ASSESSMENT RECORD

PRELUDES B, C

Group Name _____

Directions
1. For each subtest, write the goal in the appropriate column header. (Subtest goals are located at the bottom of each assessment.)
2. For each student and subtest, record the number of correct responses over the number of possible responses (e.g., 4/5). Circle scores of subtests not passed.
3. Using the guide on each Student Assessment Record, determine and record a Pass or a No Pass.
4. For students who do not pass, provide additional practice and retest. Record retest scores to the right of the original scores.

Student Names	Prelude Date ___	Subtest A Tracking Sounds and Picture Words Goal __/__	Subtest B Smooth and Bumpy Blending Goal __/__	Subtest C Comprehension Goal __/__	Prelude Date ___	Subtest A Tracking Sounds and Picture Words Goal __/__	Subtest B Smooth and Bumpy Blending Goal __/__	Subtest C Comprehension Goal __/__
	P / NP				P / NP			
	P / NP				P / NP			
	P / NP				P / NP			
	P / NP				P / NP			
	P / NP				P / NP			
	P / NP				P / NP			
	P / NP				P / NP			
	P / NP				P / NP			
	P / NP				P / NP			
	P / NP				P / NP			
	P / NP				P / NP			

©2008 Sopris West Educational Services. All rights reserved.

Blackline Master

GROUP ASSESSMENT RECORD

UNIT 1

Group Name _____

Directions

1. For each subtest, write the goal in the appropriate column header. (Subtest goals are located at the bottom of each assessment.)
2. For each student and subtest, record the number of correct responses over the number of possible responses (e.g., 4/5). Circle scores of subtests not passed.
3. Using the guide on each Student Assessment Record, determine and record a Pass or a No Pass.
4. For students who do not pass, provide additional practice and retest. Record retest scores to the right of the original scores.

Student Names	Unit ____ Date ____	Subtest A Sounds and Words Goal __/__	Subtest B Smooth and Bumpy Blending Goal __/__	Subtest C Finger Tracking Goal __/__	Unit ____ Date ____	Subtest A Sounds and Words Goal __/__	Subtest B Smooth and Bumpy Blending Goal __/__	Subtest C Finger Tracking Goal __/__
	P / NP				P / NP			
	P / NP				P / NP			
	P / NP				P / NP			
	P / NP				P / NP			
	P / NP				P / NP			
	P / NP				P / NP			
	P / NP				P / NP			
	P / NP				P / NP			
	P / NP				P / NP			
	P / NP				P / NP			

Blackline Master

©2008 Sopris West Educational Services. All rights reserved.

GROUP ASSESSMENT RECORD — UNITS 2–4

Group Name _____

Directions
1. For each subtest, write the goal in the appropriate column header. (Subtest goals are located at the bottom of each assessment.)
2. For each student and subtest, record the number of correct responses over the number of possible responses (e.g., 4/5). Circle scores of subtests not passed.
3. Using the guide on each Student Assessment Record, determine and record a Pass or a No Pass.
4. For students who do not pass, provide additional practice and retest. Record retest scores to the right of the original scores.

Student Names	Unit ___ Date ___	Subtest A Sounds Goal __/__	Subtest B Smooth and Bumpy Blending Goal __/__	Subtest C Tricky Words (and I'm) Goal __/__	Subtest D Sentences Goal __/__	Unit ___ Date ___	Subtest A Sounds Goal __/__	Subtest B Smooth and Bumpy Blending Goal __/__	Subtest C Tricky Words (and I'm) Goal __/__	Subtest D Sentences Goal __/__
	P / NP					P / NP				
	P / NP					P / NP				
	P / NP					P / NP				
	P / NP					P / NP				
	P / NP					P / NP				
	P / NP					P / NP				
	P / NP					P / NP				
	P / NP					P / NP				
	P / NP					P / NP				
	P / NP					P / NP				

©2008 Sopris West Educational Services. All rights reserved.

GROUP ASSESSMENT RECORD — UNIT 5

Directions

1. For each subtest, write the goal in the appropriate column header. (Subtest goals are located at the bottom of each assessment.)
2. For each student and subtest, record the number of correct responses over the number of possible responses (e.g., 4/5). Circle scores of subtests not passed.
3. Using the guide on each Student Assessment Record, determine and record a Pass or a No Pass.
4. For students who do not pass, provide additional practice and retest. Record retest scores to the right of the original scores.

Group Name _____

Student Names	Unit ___ Date ___	Subtest A Sounds Goal ___	Subtest B Smooth and Bumpy Blending Goal ___	Subtest C Smooth Bentlending Goal ___	Subtest D Tricky Words Goal ___	Subtest E Sentences Goal ___	Unit ___ Date ___	Subtest A Sounds Goal ___	Subtest B Smooth and Bumpy Blending Goal ___	Subtest C Smooth Blending Goal ___	Subtest D Tricky Words Goal ___	Subtest E Sentences Goal ___
	P / NP						P / NP					
	P / NP						P / NP					
	P / NP						P / NP					
	P / NP						P / NP					
	P / NP						P / NP					
	P / NP						P / NP					
	P / NP						P / NP					
	P / NP						P / NP					
	P / NP						P / NP					
	P / NP						P / NP					
	P / NP						P / NP					

GROUP ASSESSMENT RECORD

UNITS 6–8

Directions

Group Name _____

1. For each subtest, write the goal in the appropriate column header. (Subtest goals are located at the bottom of each assessment.)
2. For each student and subtest, record the number of correct responses over the number of possible responses (e.g., 4/5). Circle scores of subtests not passed.
3. For the Sentence Fluency score (last column), record the number of seconds it takes the student to complete the sentence reading. Circle scores that do not meet the desired fluency goal.
4. Using the guide on each Student Assessment Record, determine and record a Strong Pass, Weak Pass, or a No Pass.
5. For students who do not pass, provide additional practice and retest. Record retest scores to the right of the original scores.

Student Names	Unit ___ Date ___	Subtest A Sounds Goal __/__	Subtest B Smooth and Bumpy Blending Goal __/__	Subtest C Smooth Blending Goal __/__	Subtest D Tricky Words Goal __/__	Subtest E Sentences Goal __/__	Sentence Fluency Fluency Goal ___ seconds
	SP / WP / NP						
	SP / WP / NP						
	SP / WP / NP						
	SP / WP / NP						
	SP / WP / NP						
	SP / WP / NP						
	SP / WP / NP						
	SP / WP / NP						
	SP / WP / NP						
	SP / WP / NP						
	SP / WP / NP						
	SP / WP / NP						

Student Names	Unit ___ Date ___	Subtest A Sounds Goal __/__	Subtest B Smooth and Bumpy Blending Goal __/__	Subtest C Smooth Blending Goal __/__	Subtest D Tricky Words Goal __/__	Subtest E Sentences Goal __/__	Sentence Fluency Fluency Goal ___ seconds
	SP / WP / NP						
	SP / WP / NP						
	SP / WP / NP						
	SP / WP / NP						
	SP / WP / NP						
	SP / WP / NP						
	SP / WP / NP						
	SP / WP / NP						
	SP / WP / NP						
	SP / WP / NP						
	SP / WP / NP						
	SP / WP / NP						

©2008 Sopris West Educational Services. All rights reserved.

Blackline Master

GROUP ASSESSMENT RECORD

UNITS 9–15

Directions

Group Name _____

1. For each subtest, write the goal in the appropriate column header. (Subtest goals are located at the bottom of each assessment.)
2. For each student and subtest, record the number of correct responses over the number of possible responses (e.g., 4/5). Circle scores of subtests not passed.
3. For the Sentence Fluency score (last column), record the number of seconds it takes the student to complete the sentence reading. Circle scores that do not meet the desired fluency goal.
4. Using the guide on each Student Assessment Record, determine and record a Strong Pass, Weak Pass, or a No Pass.
5. For students who do not pass, provide additional practice and retest. Record retest scores to the right of the original scores.

Student Names	Unit / Date	Subtest A Sounds Goal ___	Subtest B Smooth Blending Goal ___	Subtest C Tricky Words Goal ___	Subtest D Sentence Reading Goal ___	Sentence Fluency Goal ___	Unit / Date	Subtest A Sounds Goal ___	Subtest B Smooth Blending Goal ___	Subtest C Tricky Words Goal ___	Subtest D Sentence Reading Goal ___	Sentence Fluency Goal ___
	SP/WP/NP						SP/WP/NP					
	SP/WP/NP						SP/WP/NP					
	SP/WP/NP						SP/WP/NP					
	SP/WP/NP						SP/WP/NP					
	SP/WP/NP						SP/WP/NP					
	SP/WP/NP						SP/WP/NP					
	SP/WP/NP						SP/WP/NP					
	SP/WP/NP						SP/WP/NP					
	SP/WP/NP						SP/WP/NP					
	SP/WP/NP						SP/WP/NP					
	SP/WP/NP						SP/WP/NP					

Blackline Master

©2008 Sopris West Educational Services. All rights reserved.

GROUP ASSESSMENT RECORD

UNITS 16–20

Directions

1. Write the WCPM for a Strong Pass (SP) in the space provided at the top of the fifth column. (This number is found in the bottom box of the Student Assessment Record and provides an overall goal for instruction.)
2. In the third column, record the number of Tricky Words missed. (List the words at the bottom of the form for reteaching.)
3. For the Passage Accuracy Score (fourth column), record the number of errors the student made the first time he or she read through the whole passage (excluding the title). Do not count any additional errors made if the student begins reading the passage a second time.
4. For the Oral Reading Fluency Score, record the number of words read correctly in one minute minus the number of all errors made during that minute.
5. Using the guide on each Student Assessment Record, determine and record a Strong Pass, Weak Pass, or No Pass.
6. For students who do not pass, provide additional practice and retest. Record retest scores to the right of the original scores.

Group Name _____

Student Names	Unit _____ Date _____	Tricky Word Errors	Passage Accuracy Score Goal 0–2 Errors	Oral Reading Fluency Score SP Goal ____ WCPM	Unit _____ Date _____	Tricky Word Errors	Passage Accuracy Score Goal 0–2 Errors	Oral Reading Fluency Score SP Goal ____ WCPM
	SP / WP / NP				SP / WP / NP			
	SP / WP / NP				SP / WP / NP			
	SP / WP / NP				SP / WP / NP			
	SP / WP / NP				SP / WP / NP			
	SP / WP / NP				SP / WP / NP			
	SP / WP / NP				SP / WP / NP			
	SP / WP / NP				SP / WP / NP			
	SP / WP / NP				SP / WP / NP			
	SP / WP / NP				SP / WP / NP			
	SP / WP / NP				SP / WP / NP			
	SP / WP / NP				SP / WP / NP			
	SP / WP / NP				SP / WP / NP			

©2008 Sopris West Educational Services. All rights reserved.

Blackline Master